D0128244

DR FRANKENSTEIN'S HUMAN BODY BOOK

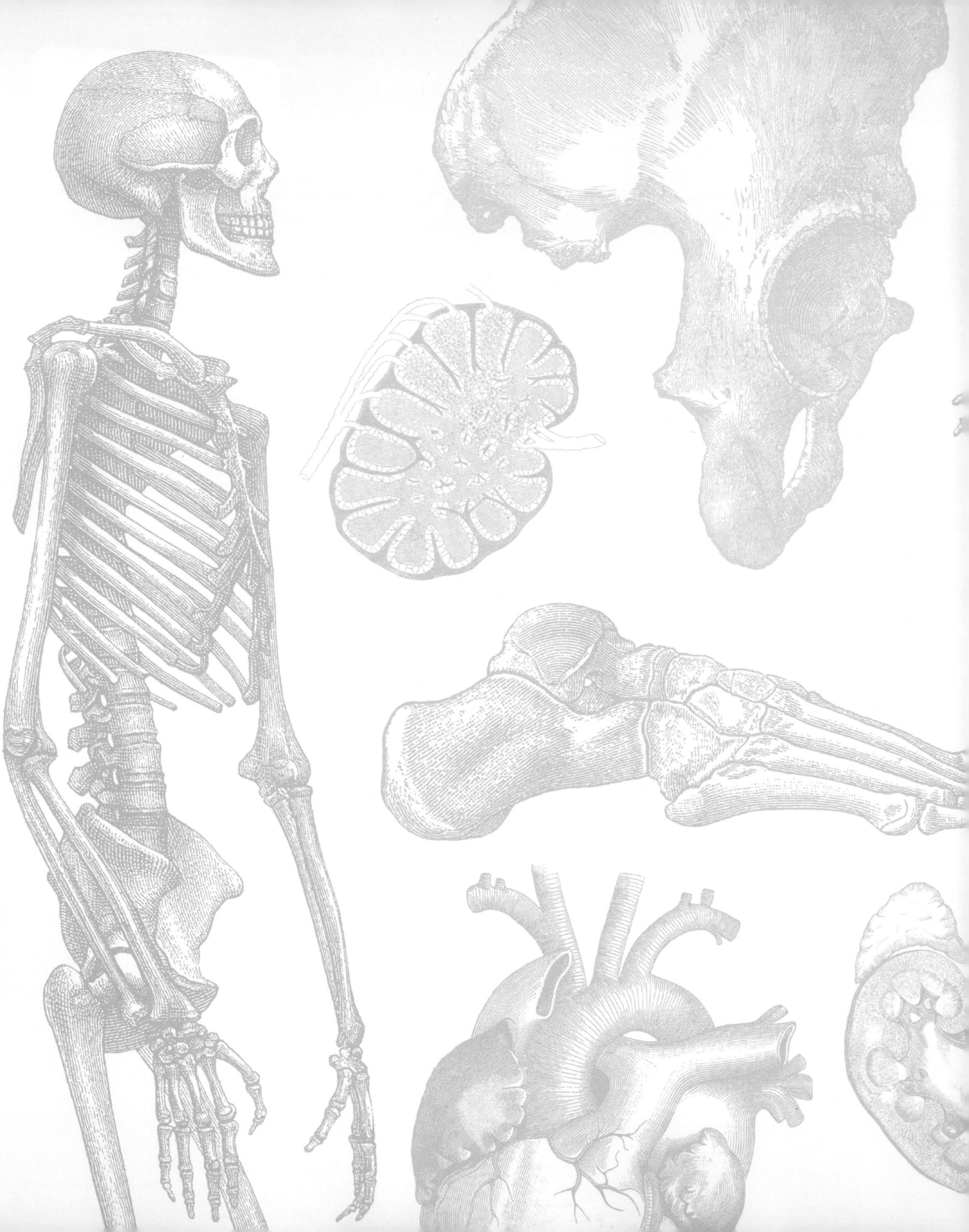

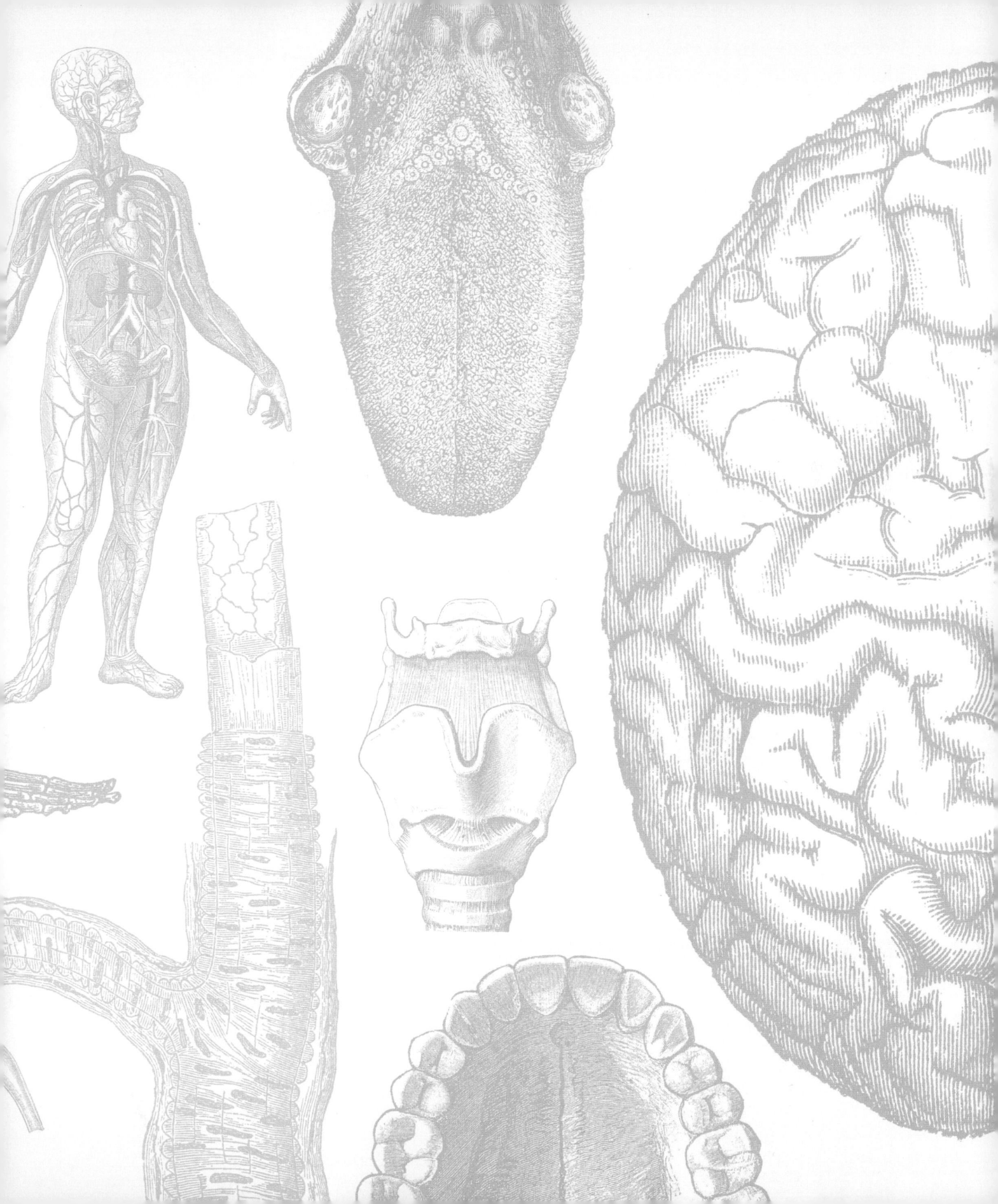

DR. FRANKENSTEIN'S HUMAN BODY BOOK

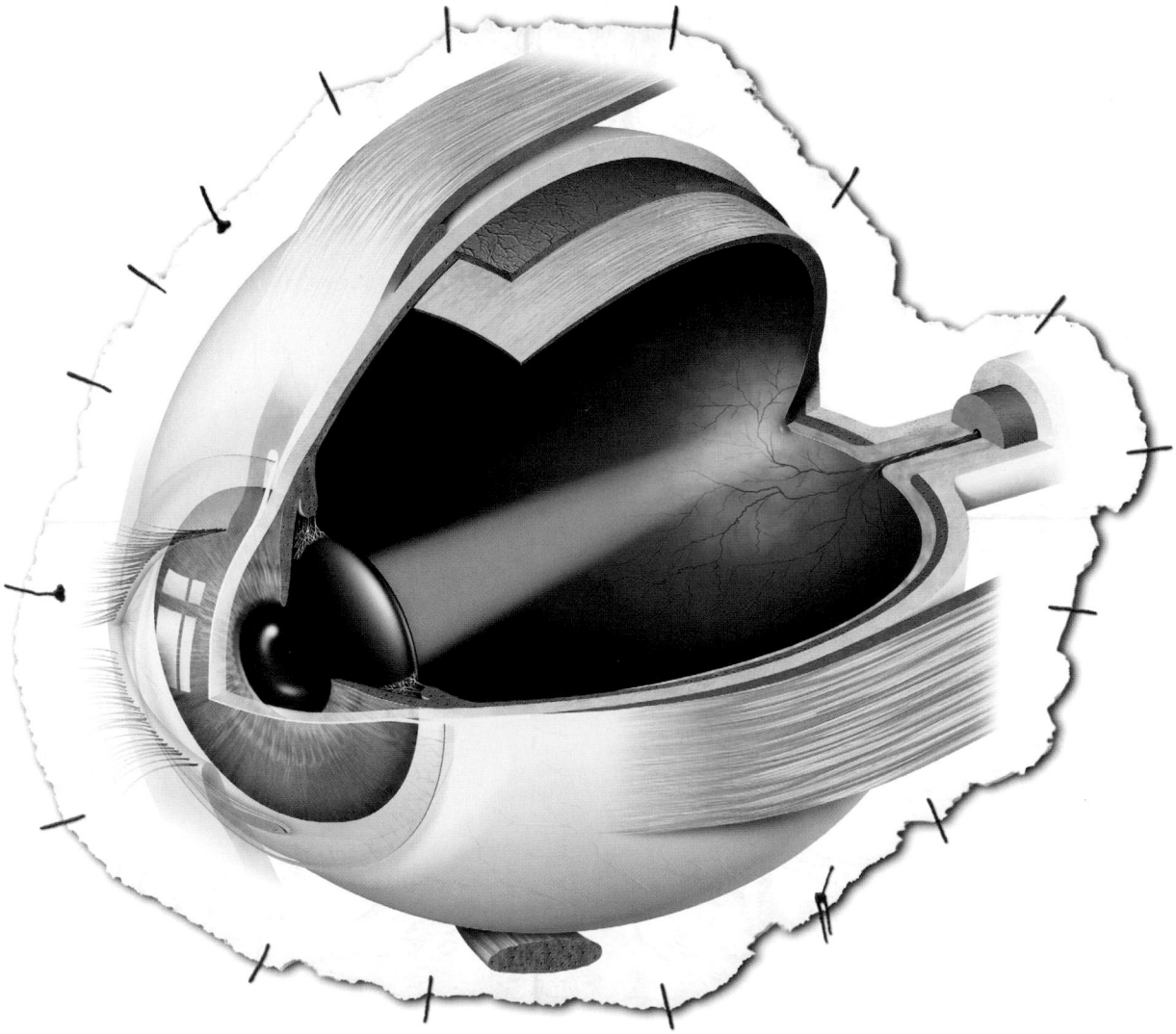

THE **MONSTROUS** TRUTH ABOUT HOW YOUR BODY WORKS

LONDON, NEW YORK, MELBOURNE,
MUNICH, AND DELHI

Author Richard Walker
Consultant Penny Preston
Artist Nick Abadzis

For Tall Tree Ltd.:
Editors Katie Dicker, Jon Richards
Designers Ed Simkins, Jonathan Vipond

For Dorling Kindersley:
Senior editor Andrea Mills
Senior art editor Philip Letsu
Managing editor Linda Esposito
Managing art editor Diane Thistlethwaite
Publishing manager Andrew Macintyre
Category publisher Laura Buller
Design development manager Sophia Tampakopoulos Turner
Production controller Angela Graef
Senior production editor Vivianne Ridgeway
Picture research Fran Vargo
Jacket editor Mariza O'Keeffe
Jacket designer Yumiko Tahata
US editor Margaret Parrish

This paperback edition published 2008
First published in the United States in 2008 by
DK Publishing 375 Hudson Street, New York, New York 10014

Copyright © 2008 Dorling Kindersley Limited
10 11 12 10 9 8 7 6 5 4 3 2
DD477—09/08

All rights reserved under International and Pan-American Copyright Conventions. No part of this publication may be reproduced, stored in a retrieval system, or transmitted in any form or by any means, electronic, mechanical, photocopying, recording, or otherwise, without the prior written permission of the copyright owner. Published in Great Britain by Dorling Kindersley Limited.

A catalog record for this book is available from the Library of Congress
ISBN: 978-0-7566-4281-5
Printed and bound by Leo Paper Products, China

Discover more at
www.dk.com

Contents

Dr. Frankenstein's masterplan..8
Raw materials 10
Tissues and organs 12
Bone basics 14
Backbone and ribs 16
Skull 18
Shoulders and arms 20
Hands 22
Pelvis 24
Legs and feet 26
Skeleton.....28
Cerebrum 30
Central nervous system 32
Nerves 34
Eyes.....36
Ears 38
Control systems 40
Blood vessels 42
Blood.....44
Heart 46
Lymph vessels and nodes.....48
Transportation systems.....50
Kidneys.....52
Urinary system.....54
Teeth 56
Mouth, throat, and esophagus....58
Stomach.....60
Intestines.....62
Liver and pancreas.....64
Digestive system.....66
Nasal cavity 68
Larynx, trachea, and bronchi 70
Lungs 72
Respiratory system 74
Arm and hand muscles.....76
Hip and leg muscles.....78
Head and neck muscles.....80
Muscular system.....82
Skin, hair, and nails.....84
The complete body.....86
Seeing inside.....88
Glossary.....90
Index and acknowledgments 92

Dr. Frankenstein's masterplan

Come inside, Dr. Frankenstein's the name. I'm sure you've heard it many times. Glad you could join me. You find me in a state of excitement. In all my years dedicated to the study of science and nature, this is the most extraordinary experiment I've ever undertaken.

As you can see, my laboratory shelves are bursting with body parts. Don't look so startled—that's everything we need to make a living, breathing human being. As my assistant, you'll be helping me every step of the way, but be warned, this is not for the faint-hearted.

Now follow me. You are about to embark on the experience of a lifetime...

Raw materials

First things first. Let's take a look at the raw materials needed to make a person. The simplest are incredibly tiny particles called atoms. They're used to make molecules that, in turn, build cells, the living units from which the body will be constructed.

light microscope

It would be impossible to see cells if it weren't for the microscope. A light microscope like this one can magnify a cell so you can see its basic features. But we need a more powerful instrument—an electron microscope—to reveal a cell's structure.

Cell membrane *surrounds cell and controls what substances enter and leave it*

atoms and molecules

It takes trillions of atoms, arranged in a highly organized fashion, to make a body. Of the 20 different types of atom inside us, the top six are oxygen, carbon, hydrogen, nitrogen, calcium, and phosphorus. Atoms can exist on their own, but most prefer to link up and form molecules, such as water molecules, which can make up to 60 percent of a human's body weight.

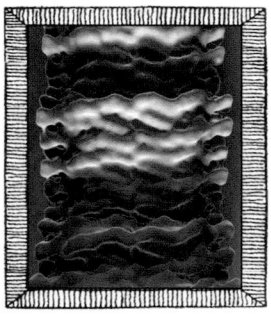

A cell membrane *has two layers of molecules containing carbon, hydrogen, oxygen, nitrogen, and phosphorus atoms.*

A water molecule *is made of two hydrogen atoms (red) and one oxygen atom (yellow).*

Cytoplasm *is a jellylike fluid in which organelles float*

Day 1

This is history in the making. With the help of my new assistant, I can realize my dream—creating a human body. Assistant seems eager and enthusiastic. Has grasped the basics, assembled atoms, and surveyed cells. Now let's build some tissues.

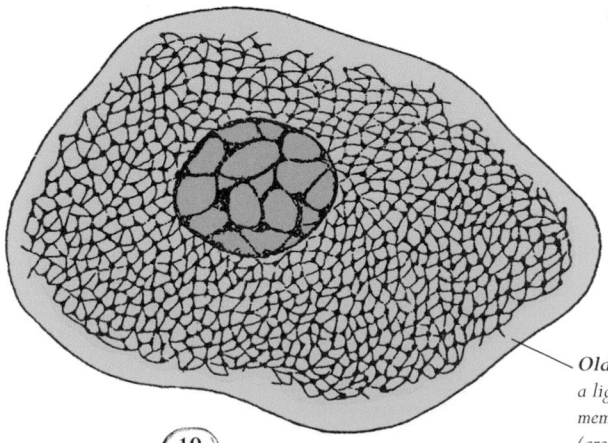

Old drawing of a cell*, as seen with a light microscope, shows a thin cell membrane surrounding the cytoplasm (green and brown), and the nucleus (purple)*

cells and organelles

Though tiny, cells are far from simple. Look carefully and you'll see that in between the cell membrane and the nucleus there are lots of tiny structures, called organelles. Each of these has its own job to do, but organelles also work together to bring the cell to life.

Golgi apparatus *packages and distributes newly made proteins*

Rough endoplasmic reticulum *makes and transports proteins*

Nucleus *is the cell's control center where DNA is stored*

Mitochondrion *releases energy to power the cell's chemical reactions*

DNA and proteins

Locked away inside the nucleus of every cell are 46 extremely long DNA molecules. These DNA molecules contain the 25,000 or so instructions we'll need to make a body. These instructions—called genes—control the production of proteins (substances that are, as we'll see, in charge of organizing all the body's other molecules).

DNA molecule *consists of two long, intertwined strands that coil up for easy storage*

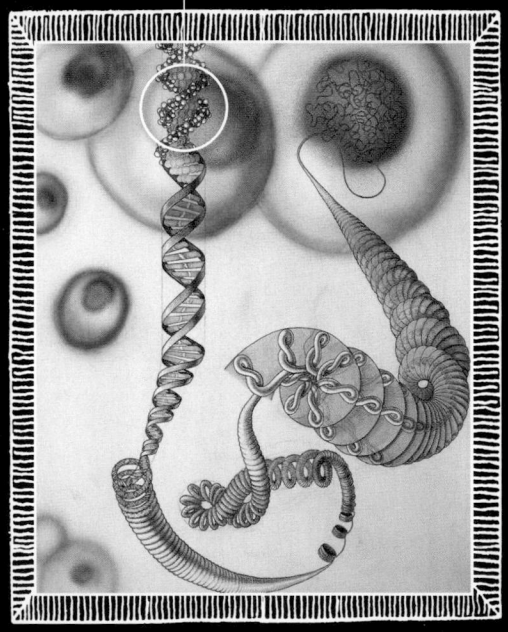

The most versatile of the body's molecules, proteins play key roles in building and running cells. The enzymes that control the chemical reactions of life are especially important. Proteins are formed from smaller molecules called amino acids.

Each type of protein *has a specific shape determined by the precise sequence of its amino acids*

Tissues and organs

Building a body takes tens of trillions of cells. There are more than 200 different types of cell, each with its own shape, size, and job to do. Cells of the same or similar types organize themselves into groups called tissues. Two or more types of tissues form organs, such as the stomach.

organs and systems

The stomach is just one of the body's many organs. Other organs include the heart and the brain. A group of linked organs make up a system, such as the digestive system.

Stomach wall *contains epithelial, connective, muscular, and nervous tissues*

organ building

Cut a thin section through the folded wall of the stomach, put it under a microscope, and this is what you see. The white space is the inside of the stomach. A thin, dark pink layer of epithelial tissue covers a thicker, pale pink layer of connective tissue. Below that is some muscle tissue. Together these tissues contribute to building the stomach.

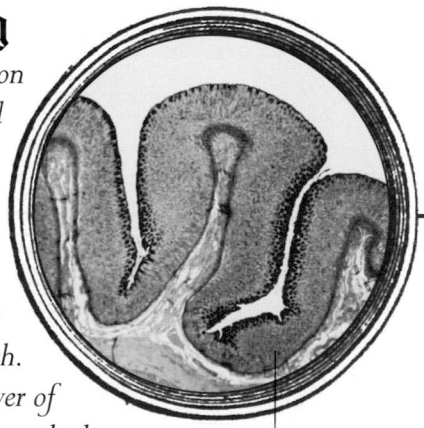

Connective tissue *in the stomach wall holds other tissues together*

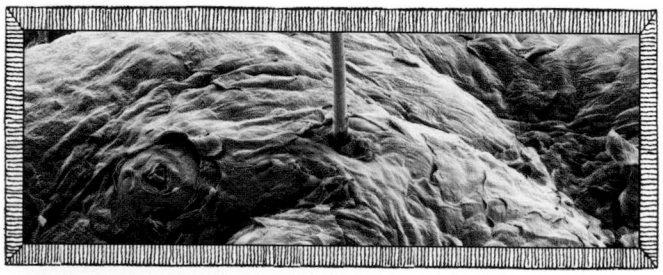

on the outside

Tissues aren't restricted to the inside of the body. This image (left), produced using a scanning electron microscope, shows the epidermis—a type of epithelial tissue—that forms the upper layer of the skin and covers the body.

line and cover

Epithelial tissue, or epithelium, is made from tightly packed cells. Epithelium lines and protects the insides (and covers the outsides) of organs that make up several body systems, such as the digestive, respiratory, and urinary systems. Touch the inside of your mouth and you are feeling epithelium. It also forms glands and the insides of blood vessels.

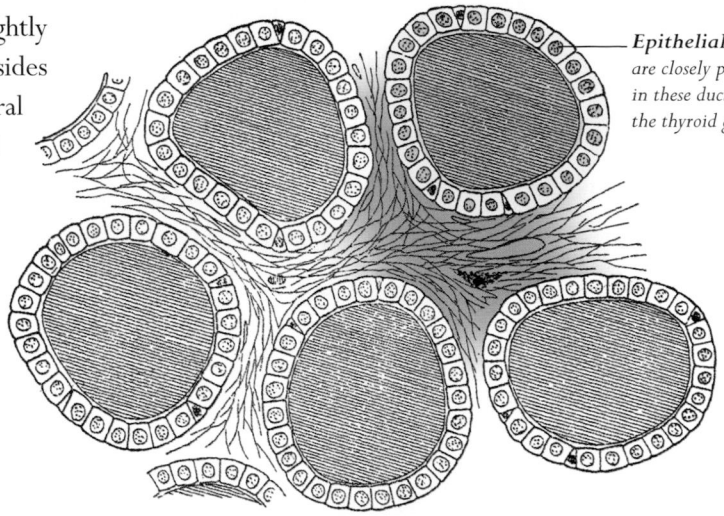

Epithelial cells *are closely packed in these ducts from the thyroid gland*

The stomach *is one of the organs that make up the digestive system*

support and package

Connective tissues include cartilage, bone, and other tissues that support the body and package its organs. They also include adipose tissue (right), which has plump fat-storing cells.

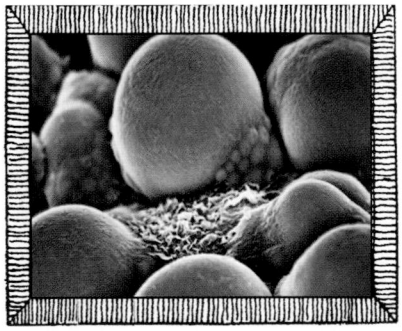

movement

Muscle tissue consists of cells that contract (get shorter) to produce movement. Skeletal muscle moves the body, smooth muscle (left) makes organs squeeze, and cardiac muscle makes the heart beat.

control

Nervous tissue is made from long, spiky cells that are linked into a massive network. They generate and carry electrical signals at high speed to control everything you do.

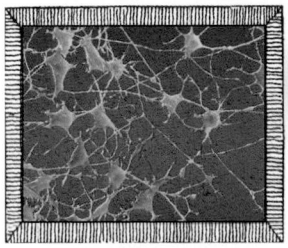

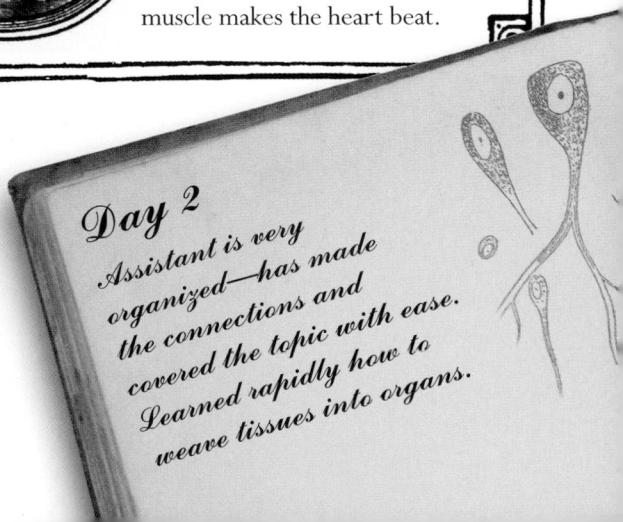

Bone basics

Time to get a grip! Grab hold of your wrist and squeeze gently. Does it collapse completely? No, because under your skin there are bones. Bones are produced from a mix of cells, mineral salts, and collagen fibers that makes them alive, hard, and strong, but not brittle. A combination of compact and spongy bone makes the skeleton as strong as steel, but a fraction of the weight.

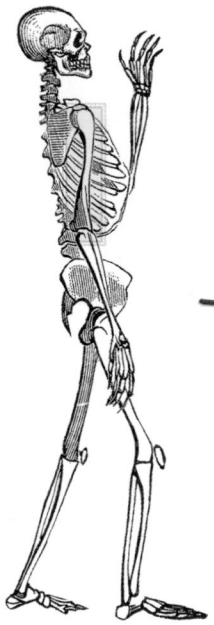

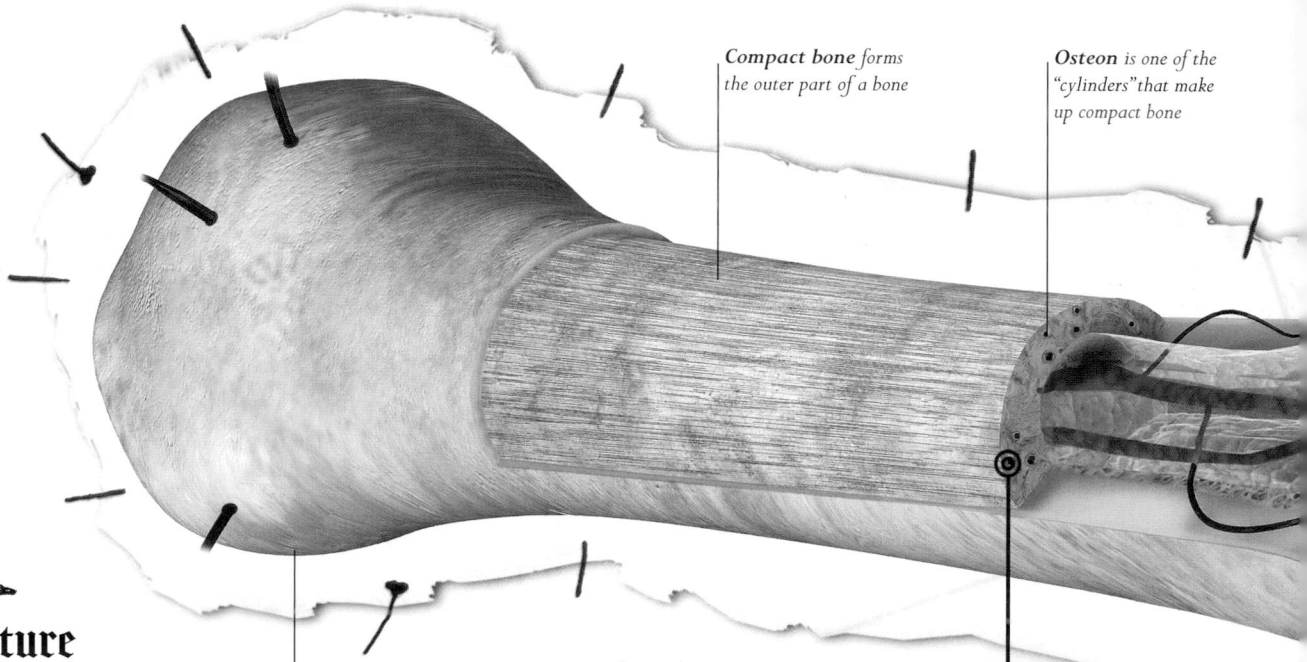

bone structure

Here you can see the inside of a long bone. It's been cut open to show the different types of bone tissue.

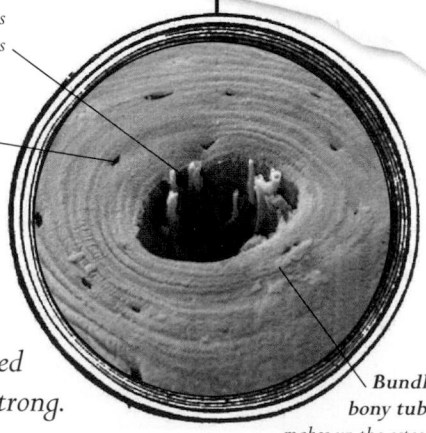

compact bone

Nearly as hard as the white enamel in your teeth, compact bone is made of weight-bearing cylinders called osteons that run in parallel down the bone. Each osteon consists of concentric tubes like the rings of a tree. This is where bone cells live in tiny spaces called lacunae. Compact bone forms a bone's outer coat and makes it very strong.

spongy bone

If your bones were made solely from compact bone, they would be so heavy that you wouldn't be able to move. Fortunately, bones also contain lighter spongy bone consisting of strong, weight-bearing struts. In some bones, the spaces between the struts are filled with red bone marrow.

bone cells

When hard bone tissue is laid down, the cells that produce it become trapped in their own creation, but remain connected to neighboring cells through narrow canals. These lonely osteocytes keep bone tissues in good shape.

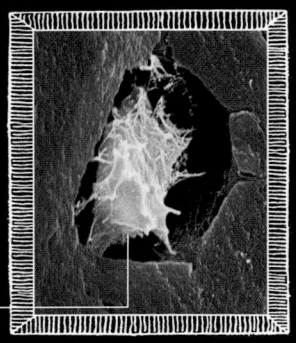

***Osteocytes** live in isolation but stay in touch with each other using their spiky processes*

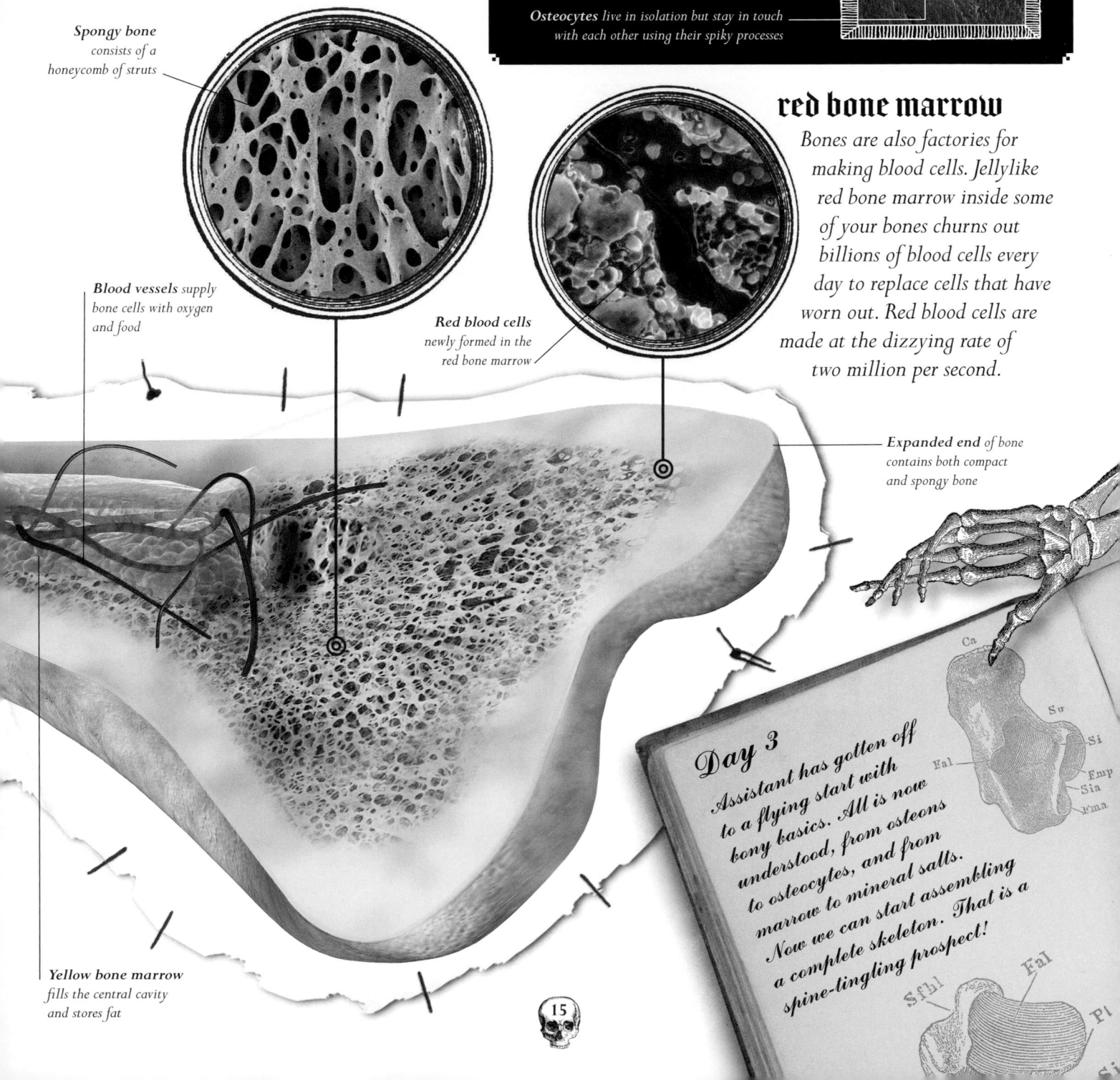

red bone marrow

Bones are also factories for making blood cells. Jellylike red bone marrow inside some of your bones churns out billions of blood cells every day to replace cells that have worn out. Red blood cells are made at the dizzying rate of two million per second.

Backbone and ribs

Whether you call it the backbone, vertebral column, or spine, this chain of bones forms the core of the skeleton. Everything else will hang from it. The S-shape of the upright spine gives it a natural springiness to absorb shocks during movement. With the backbone in place, the ribs can be added as well.

Atlas and axis *allow head to nod and shake*

Seven cervical vertebrae *support the neck and head*

Twelve thoracic vertebrae *form joints with the ribs*

Joint *between one vertebra and the next*

Intervertebral disks *(green) are easy to see in this CT scan*

disks and movement

Each vertebra's chunky body is separated from that of its neighbor by a disk of cartilage with a squishy center. These disks protect the vertebrae from sudden shocks. They also allow bending and twisting movements that, when "added up" for the whole backbone, make it fairly flexible.

Body of vertebra *carries most of the weight pressing downward*

Bony process *of vertebra*

Facet *forms joint with the end of a rib*

Four thoracic vertebrae *seen in side view*

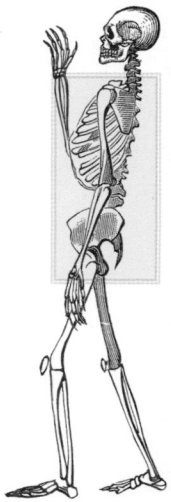

the spine

You'll see that the spine is built from a stack of 24 oddly shaped bones called vertebrae, along with a sacrum and coccyx. These four thoracic vertebrae show the basic structure of a vertebra, although they vary according to their type, position, and role.

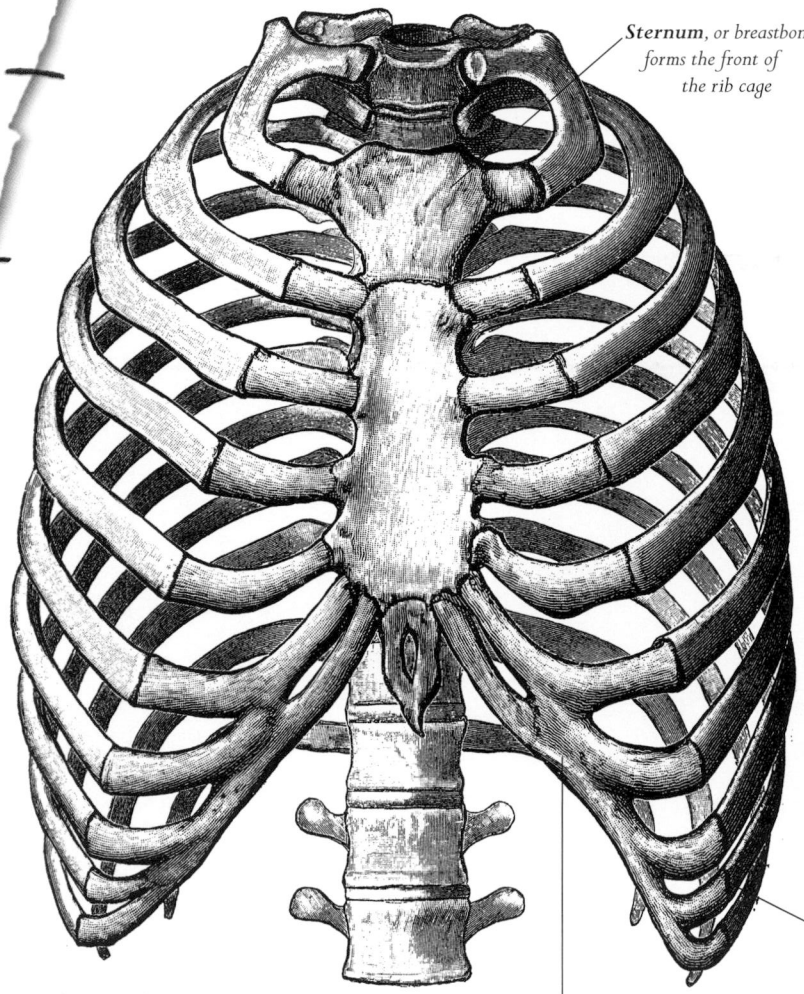

the rib cage

Now let's build a rib cage. Take 12 pairs of flattened, curved ribs and form movable joints with the thoracic vertebrae so the rib cage can move up and down. At the front, connect the upper 10 ribs to the sternum using flexible costal cartilage.

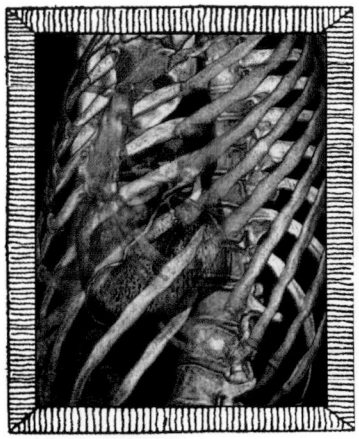

chest protection

This CT scan of a person's chest (above) shows the heart surrounded and protected by the rib cage. The rib cage also protects the lungs (not shown here).

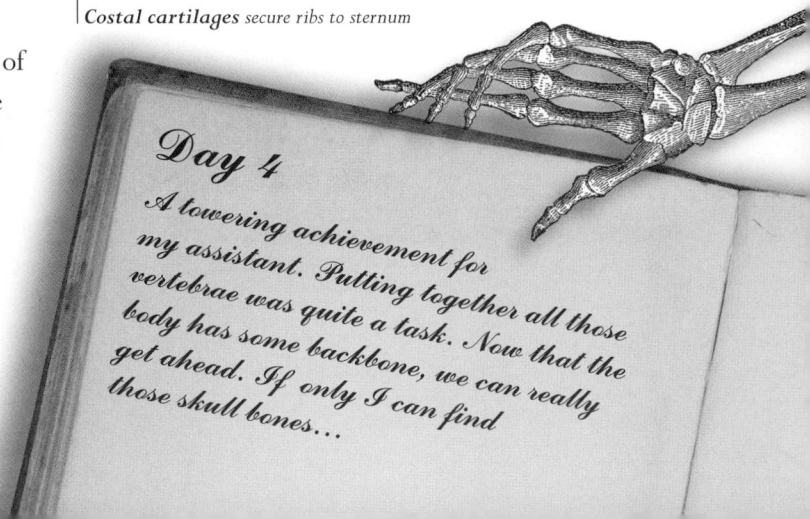

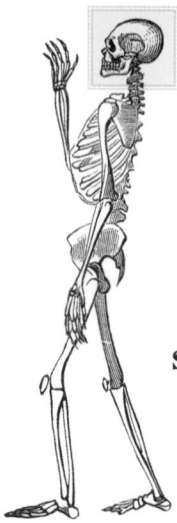

Skull

Tap gently on the side of your head and what do you feel? Just under the skin is the most complex part of your skeleton—the skull. It's really important because it protects the brain, eyes, ears, tongue, and nose. The skull also helps to determine what the face looks like.

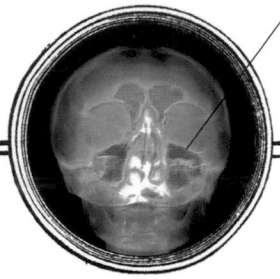

Skull X-ray *shows two pairs of sinuses (orange)*

losing weight

Some of the skull bones around the eye sockets contain hollow, air-filled spaces called sinuses. They make the skull a bit lighter in weight so it doesn't push down so much on the backbone. The sinuses are connected to the nose, so they also help moisten and warm breathed-in air.

Suture *between frontal and parietal bones*

Frontal bone *forms the front part of the cranium and shapes the forehead*

Temporal bone *forms part of the side of the cranium*

Maxillae *form the upper jaw*

Mandible *is the only skull bone that moves freely*

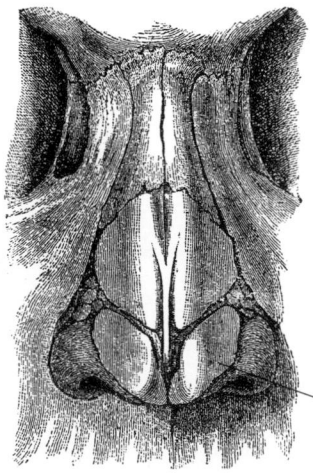

Alar cartilage *is one of several plates of cartilage that shape the nose*

bendy nose

Bone isn't the only material used in the skeleton. Tough but flexible cartilage is found on bone ends, in ear flaps, and in the nose—give yours a tweak to feel it.

locked together

Joints called sutures give the skull extra strength, locking the skull bones together like pieces in a jigsaw puzzle. Only the mandible moves to let you eat, drink, speak, and breathe.

bones of the skull

Here are the 28 bones—including six tiny ear bones—you'll need to construct a skull. The frontal, occipital, sphenoid, and ethmoid bones, plus the paired parietal and temporal bones, form the domed cranium around the brain. Fourteen bones form the framework of the face.

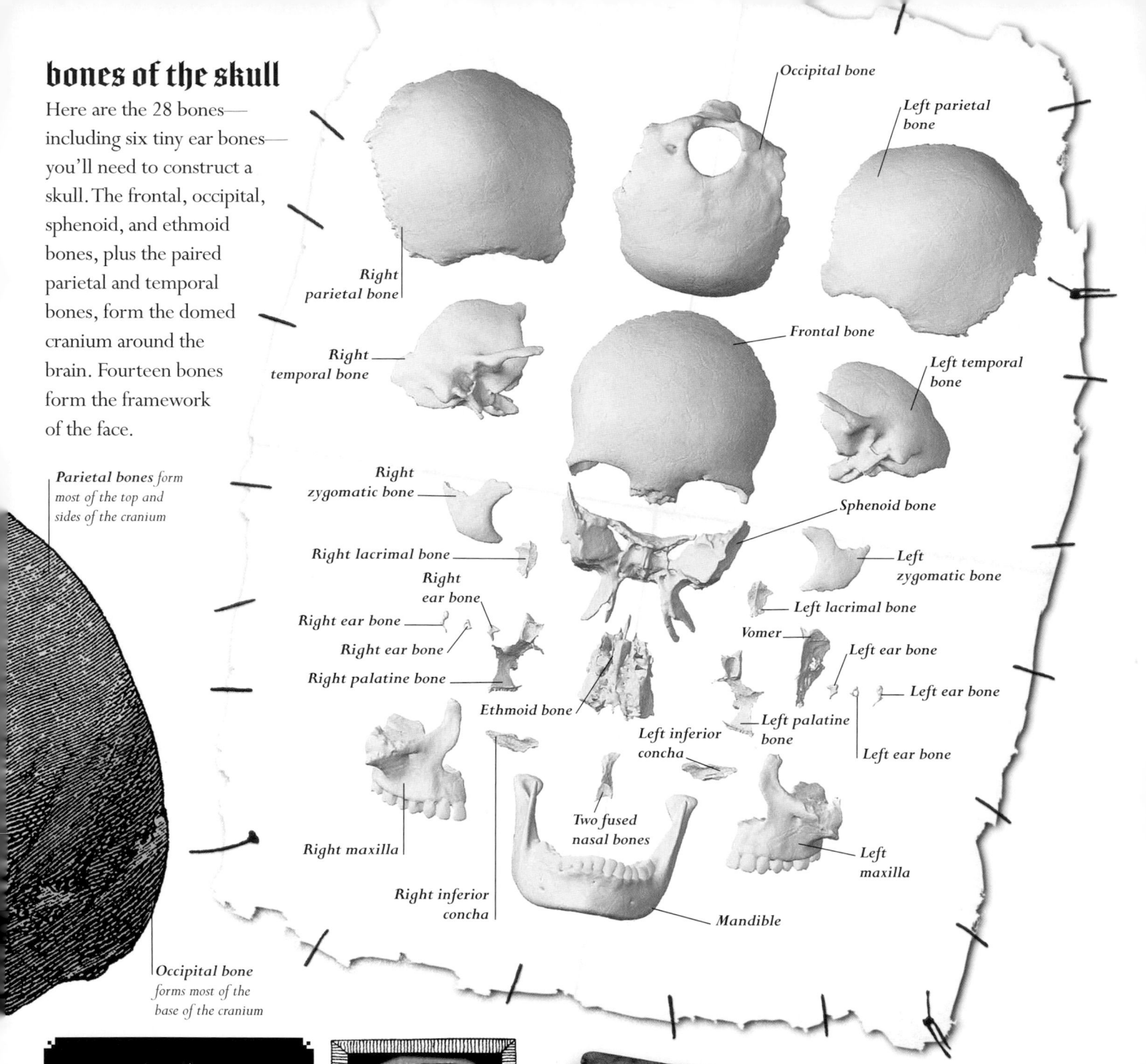

inside the skull

In this CT scan (right) the top of the skull has been "removed" to reveal the space normally occupied by the brain.

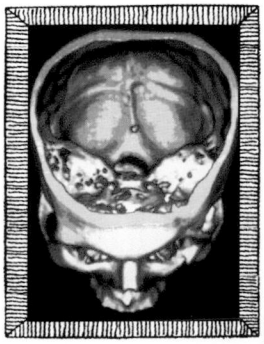

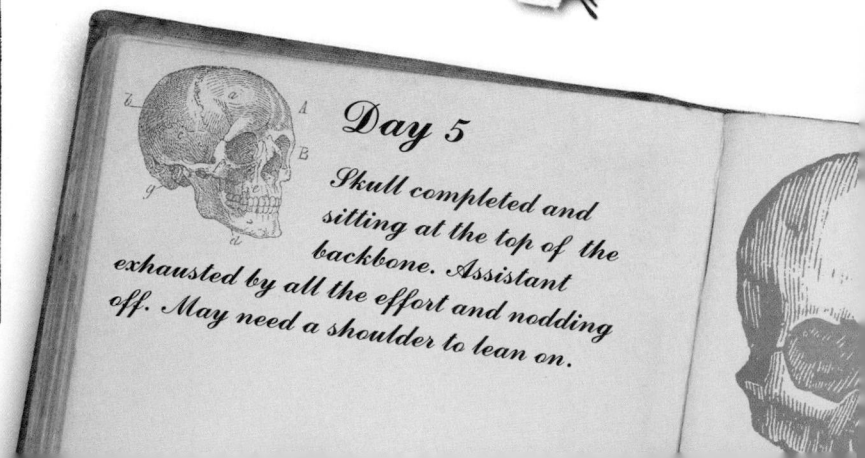

Shoulders and arms

The time has come to add the highly versatile upper limbs to our growing skeleton. The shoulder blade fits onto the back of the rib cage, providing a handy joint to attach the upper arm bone (humerus). The humerus is linked to the two bones of the forearm (radius and ulna).

shoulder joint

This is the body's most freely moving joint. It's a ball-and-socket joint that allows movement in any direction. But that freedom comes at a price. The joint has to be held in place by all sorts of ligaments, muscles, and tendons.

Head of humerus *forms the "ball" of the shoulder joint*

Scapula*, or shoulder blade, is flat and triangular*

Cavity in scapula *forms ball-and-socket joint with head of the humerus*

Humerus

Ball-and-socket joint *contains a bone with a ball-shaped head that fits into a rounded socket. The ball is free to rotate in any direction.*

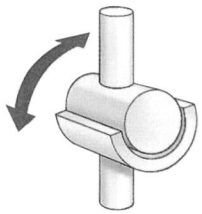

Hinge joint *has a bone with a cylindrical head that fits in a half-pipe-shaped socket. The bone can move back and forward at one angle only.*

flexible arms

The combination of a ball-and-socket joint at the shoulder, a hinge joint in the elbow, and pivot joints at either end of the forearm, gives the arm great flexibility. The pivot joints let the bones rotate over each other, allowing you to twist your hand.

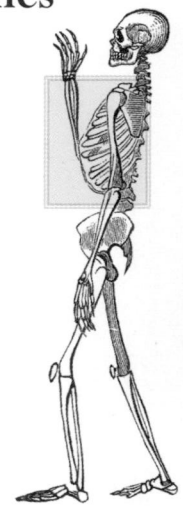

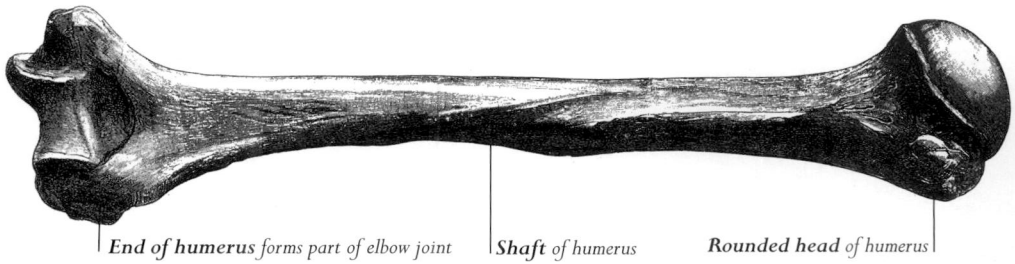

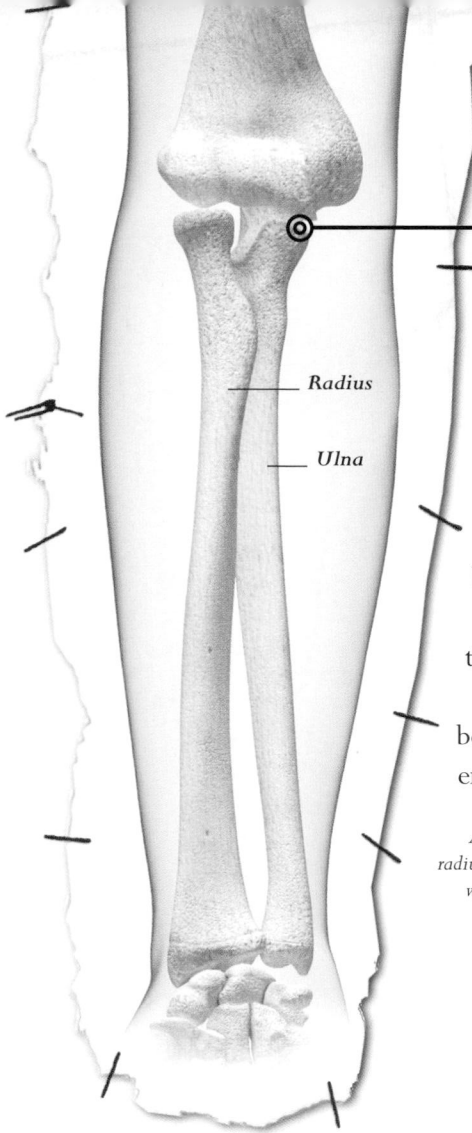

elbow joint

As you can see in this X-ray, the ulna and radius form a hinge at the elbow. A hinge joint only allows the arm to bend or straighten at the elbow, just as a door can only open or close.

break and repair

In case you break any bones—such as this ulna and radius—you should know that they have a built-in repair system. A cast, or pins, may be needed to ensure the bone ends line up and heal properly.

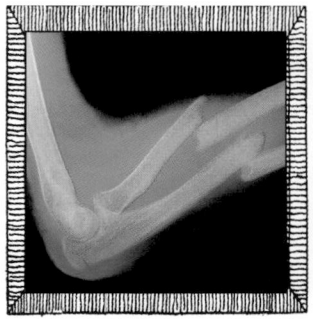

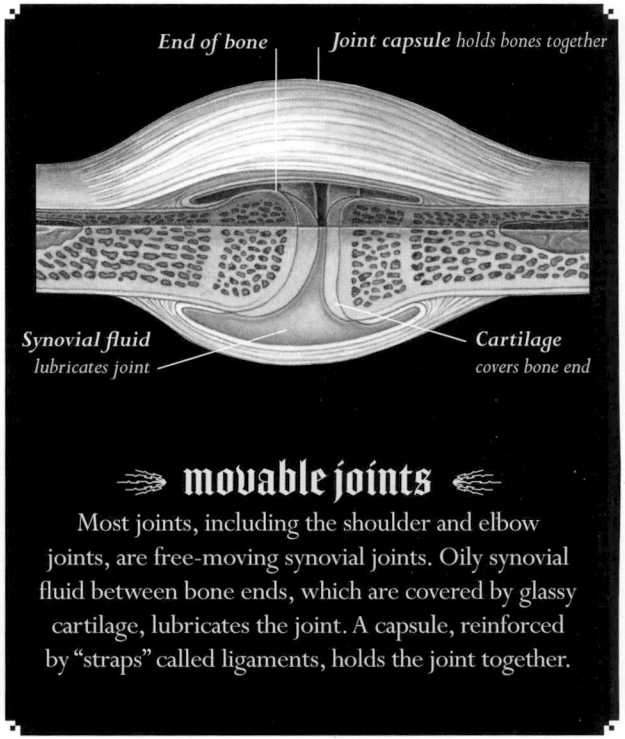

movable joints

Most joints, including the shoulder and elbow joints, are free-moving synovial joints. Oily synovial fluid between bone ends, which are covered by glassy cartilage, lubricates the joint. A capsule, reinforced by "straps" called ligaments, holds the joint together.

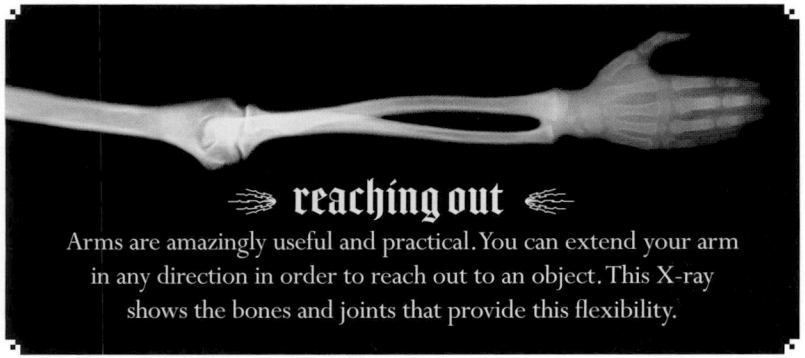

reaching out

Arms are amazingly useful and practical. You can extend your arm in any direction in order to reach out to an object. This X-ray shows the bones and joints that provide this flexibility.

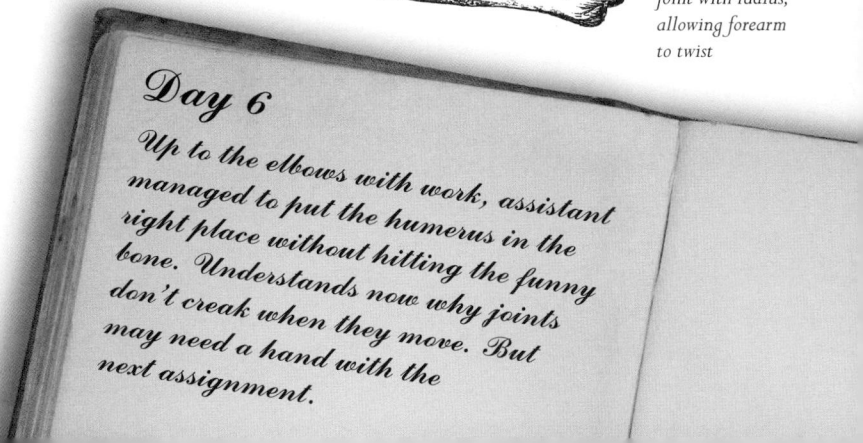

Hands

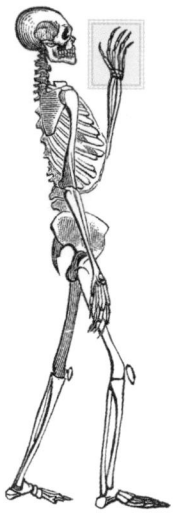

The hands are made from lots of small bones with flexible joints. Hinged loosely at the end of the forearm, the hand can perform a range of movements. In particular, the thumb and fingers can grasp and manipulate objects. That's why the hands are so useful to my assistant!

flexible thumb

Of the five digits, the thumb is the most mobile. Thanks to a saddle joint at its base, where metacarpal meets carpal, the thumb can move across the palm of the hand and then turn inward to touch or oppose the tips of each of the fingers, as you can see in this X-ray.

Condyloid joint *between metacarpal and phalanx (finger bone)*

Thumb*, or first digit, has only two phalanges*

Carpal bones*, together with the ends of the forearm bones, form the wrist*

Plane joint *between carpal bones*

Metacarpal bones *form the palm of the hand*

A saddle joint *is very flexible, with bone ends that fit together like two saddles.*

A plane joint *forms where bone surfaces are nearly flat and allows only limited movement.*

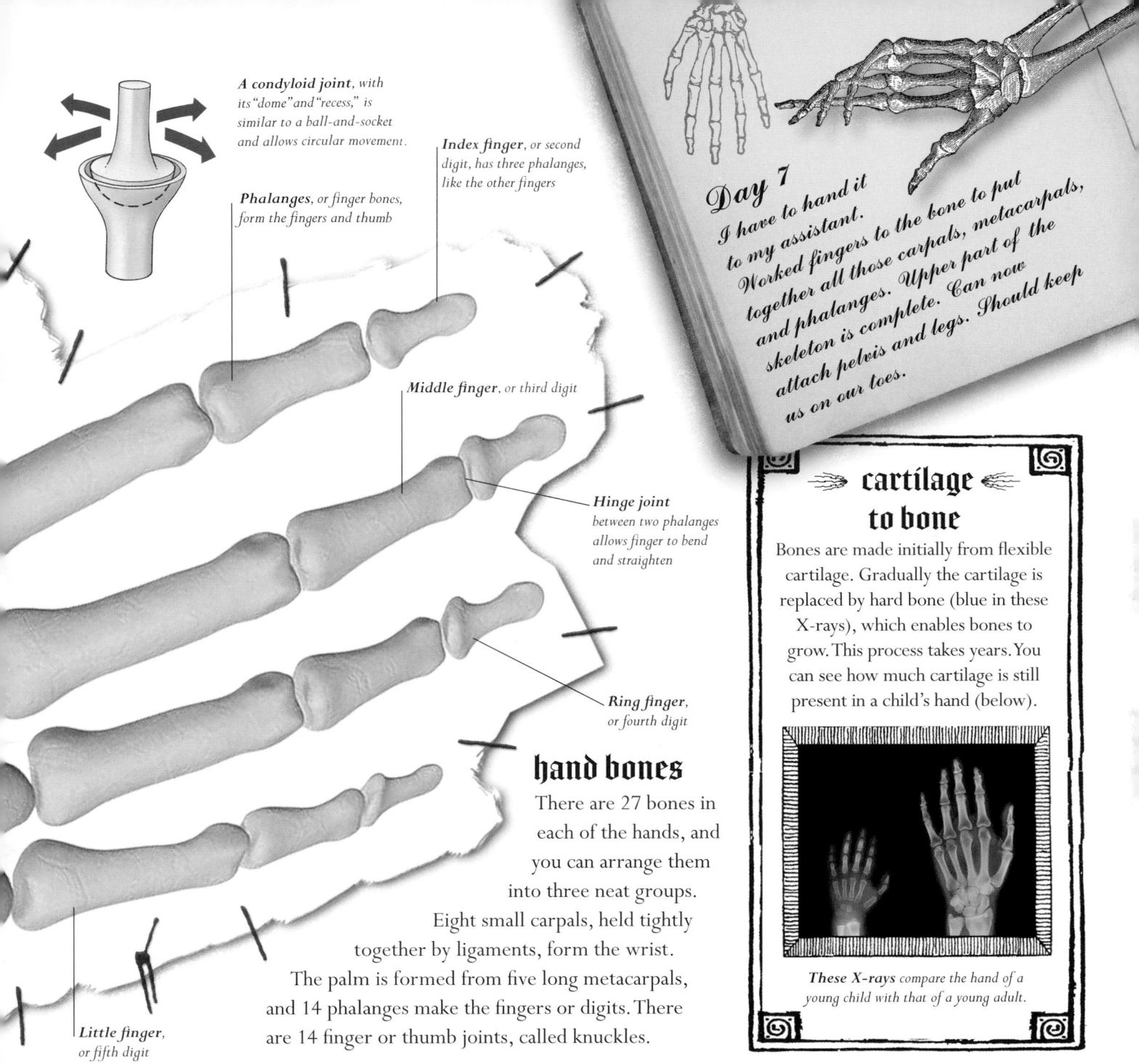

hand bones

There are 27 bones in each of the hands, and you can arrange them into three neat groups. Eight small carpals, held tightly together by ligaments, form the wrist. The palm is formed from five long metacarpals, and 14 phalanges make the fingers or digits. There are 14 finger or thumb joints, called knuckles.

cartilage to bone

Bones are made initially from flexible cartilage. Gradually the cartilage is replaced by hard bone (blue in these X-rays), which enables bones to grow. This process takes years. You can see how much cartilage is still present in a child's hand (below).

These X-rays *compare the hand of a young child with that of a young adult.*

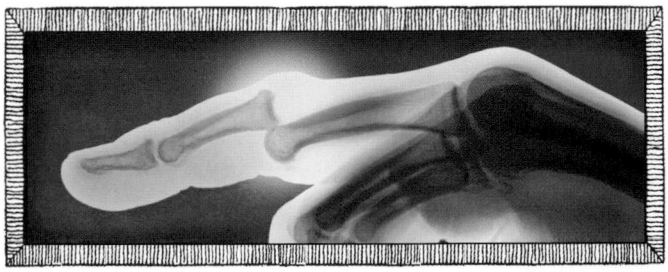

disconnected

A fall or other injury can force bones out of line so they become dislocated like these X-rayed finger bones (left). Surrounding nerves and ligaments may also be damaged. A doctor can manipulate the bones back to their correct positions.

Pelvis

Put your hands on your hips and you will feel your pelvis. This vital component anchors the legs to the backbone—so when you run in one direction, the rest of your body follows. The pelvis also supports the organs found in the abdomen, the area between the chest and the tops of the legs.

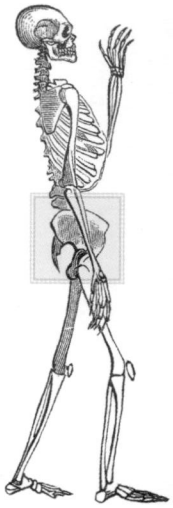

Crest of iliac bone *where you "put your hands on your hips"*

Acetabulum *is the deep socket into which the rounded head of the femur fits*

Ischium *forms the rear part of the hip bone and carries your weight when you sit*

Pubis *forms the front of the hip bone*

INSIDE VIEW

Pubis

Ischium

OUTSIDE VIEW

hip bones

When you were younger, each of your hip bones consisted of three separate bones called the ilium, ischium, and pubis. But as we get older, these bones fuse together into a single unit.

Illium *is the largest of the three bones making a hip bone*

leg link

The hip joint is formed where the "ball" of the thigh bone, or femur, meets the "socket" in the hip bone. This ball-and-socket joint is less flexible than the shoulder joint. The bones are held together by ligaments when you walk, run, or jump.

Ball-and-socket joint *between hip bone and femur*

Strong ligaments *hold hip joint together and prevent bones separating*

Femur

bony pelvis

Put the two hip bones together and you make the pelvic girdle. At the front, they meet at a slightly movable cartilage joint called the pubic symphysis. At the rear, they are anchored to the sacrum. The hip bones, sacrum, and coccyx form the bowl-shaped pelvis.

***Sacrum**, part of the backbone, is attached to the two hip bones*

Ilium

***Joint** between the sacrum and hip bone is stabilized by strong ligaments*

***Pelvic inlet** is central space of pelvis*

***Pubic symphysis** is where two hip bones are joined by a cartilage disk*

Pubis

Ischium

MALE PELVIS

***X-ray** showing the artificial components (pink) of a hip joint*

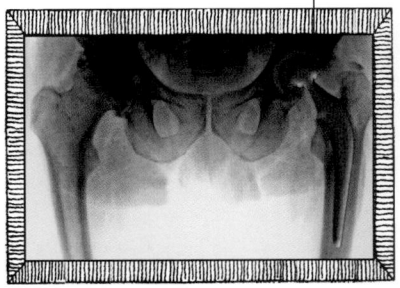

artificial joint

Joints damaged by injury or disease can be replaced. The ends of damaged bones are removed and replacement parts made of metal or plastic are inserted. A hip replacement is now a very common surgical procedure.

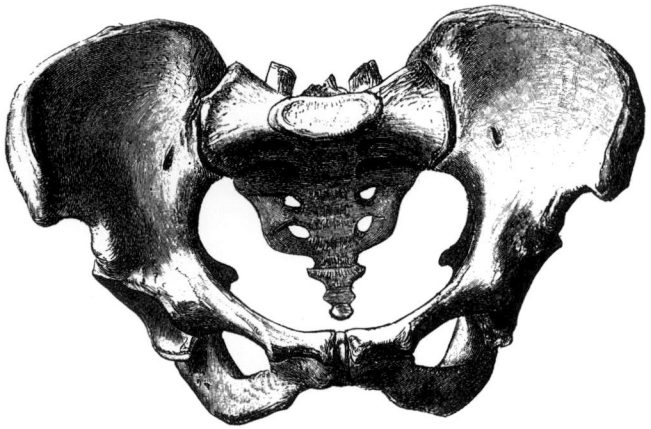

FEMALE PELVIS

male and female

It's time to check we're using the right pelvis for our creation. A man's pelvis is narrower and deeper than a woman's pelvis. A woman's pelvis has a wider pelvic inlet (opening). This allows space for a baby's head to go through when she gives birth.

Legs and feet

Today's task is to assemble the bones of the legs and feet. They support the body and push it off the ground when you walk or run. One interesting design point: when the body is upright, the knees go into a "locked" position to save energy.

knee joint

Located where the femur and tibia meet, the knee joint is a special kind of hinge joint that allows the leg to bend and straighten, but also rotate a little. Ligaments inside and outside the joint reinforce it. Cartilage inside the joint stabilizes it.

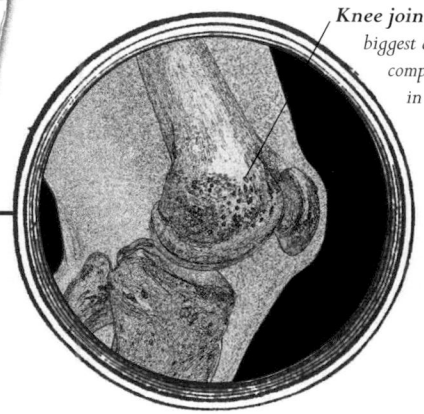

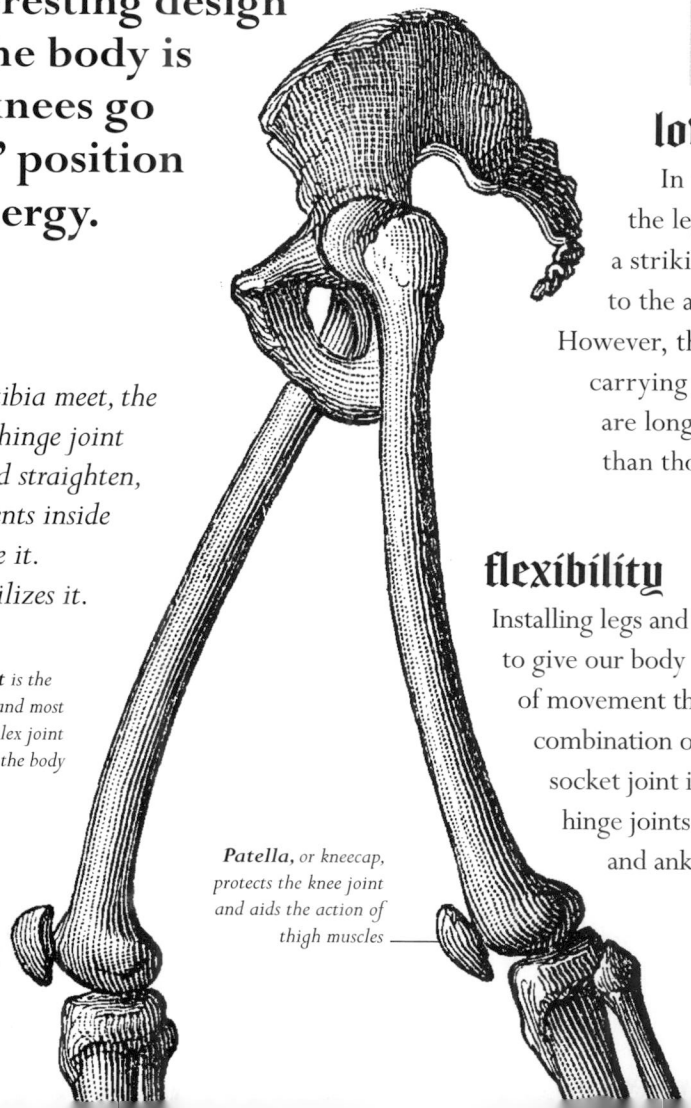

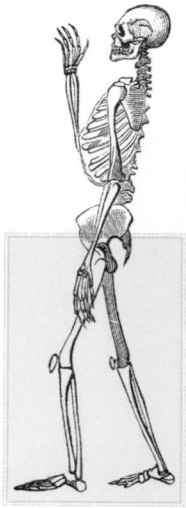

lower limbs

In terms of bones, the legs and feet bear a striking resemblance to the arms and hands. However, the leg bones are carrying weight, so they are longer and stronger than those in the arms.

flexibility

Installing legs and feet is going to give our body a great variety of movement thanks to the combination of a ball-and-socket joint in the hip, and hinge joints at the knee and ankle.

push up

This X-ray shows the position of the foot bones if you stand on tiptoe. Only the toe bones remain in contact with the ground.

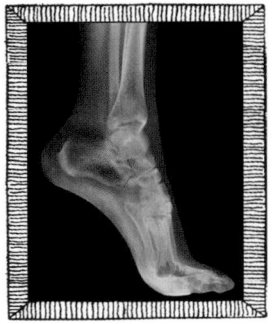

***X-ray** of foot on tiptoe*

the foot

Each foot is made from 26 bones organized as seven tarsals, five metatarsals, and 14 phalanges. The arrangement is similar to the hands, but the feet are less flexible because the toes are short, and strong ligaments bind the bones together. The foot forms a strong base for standing and running. This platform is also curved, giving added springiness during movement.

***Fibula** is the smaller of the lower leg bones*

***Tibia**, or shin bone, runs from the knee to the ankle*

Ankle joint

***Calcaneus**, or heel bone*

***Metatarsals**, or sole bones*

***Phalanges**, or toe bones*

***Little toe**, or fifth digit*

***Fourth toe** or digit*

***Third toe** or digit*

***Second toe** or digit*

***Big toe**, or first digit*

***Talus** forms joint with tibia and fibula at the ankle*

***Tarsals** form the rear of the foot*

extra help

This X-ray of the ankle (below) shows how the broken parts of a fractured fibula have been pinned together. These pins ensure that the bone stays the right shape while it is healing.

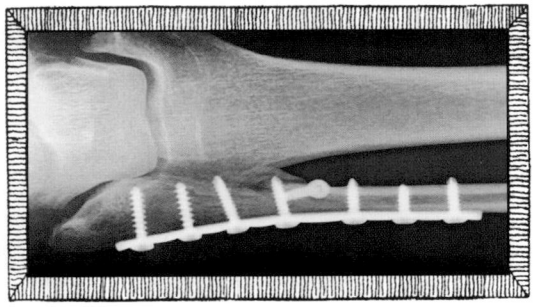

Skeleton

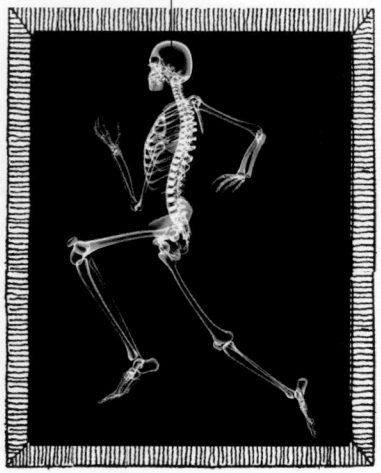

A skeleton in motion shows how flexible it is

Thanks to some sterling work, we have now put the 206 bones in place, together with joints and ligaments, to make an entire skeleton. With this movable scaffolding in position, anything is possible. We could add muscles to move those bones—but that's for the future. You should now check that your knowledge of the skeleton is complete.

support and movement

Here's your checklist of what the skeleton does for the body. It provides support, protects internal organs, and allows the body to move in lots of different ways.

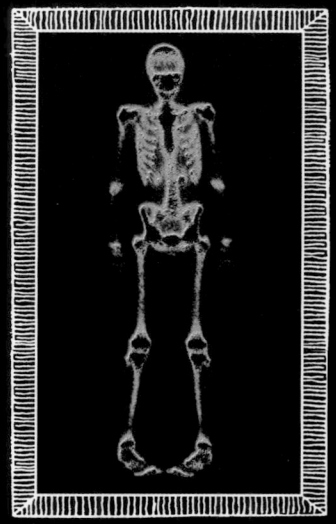

A radionuclide, or gamma scan, of the skeleton from the back.

bone scan

This is a different way of looking at bones. An injected radioactive chemical is taken up by bone cells and reveals, in a scan, which parts of the skeleton are more active (red) or less active (blue).

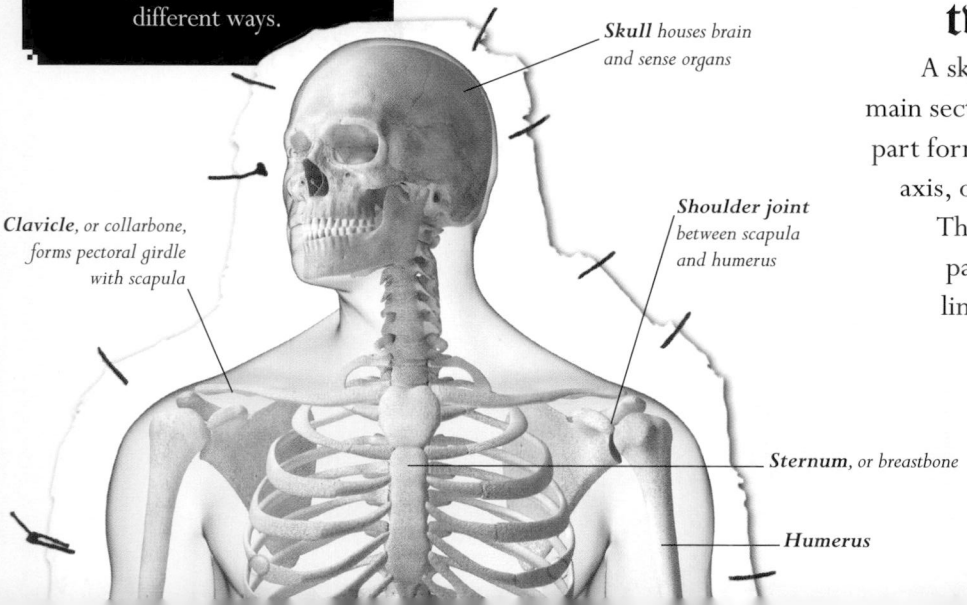

two in one

A skeleton has two main sections. The axial part forms the core, or axis, of the skeleton. The appendicular part attaches the limbs to the axis.

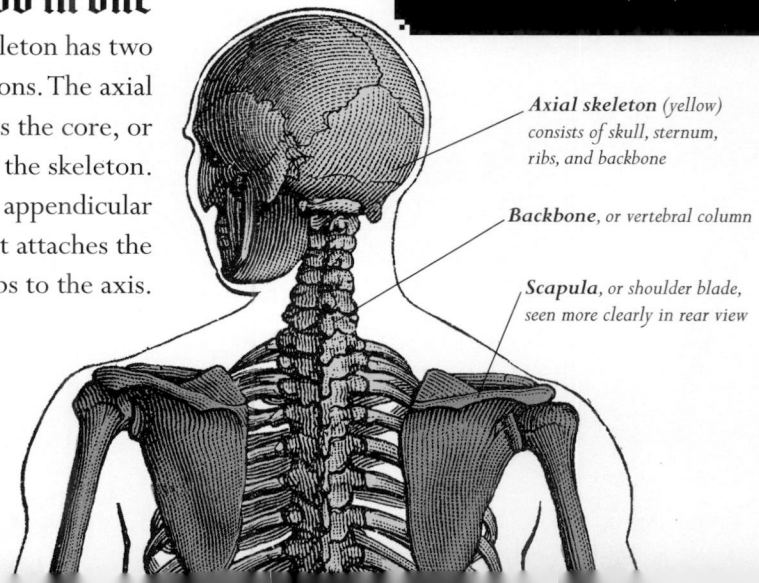

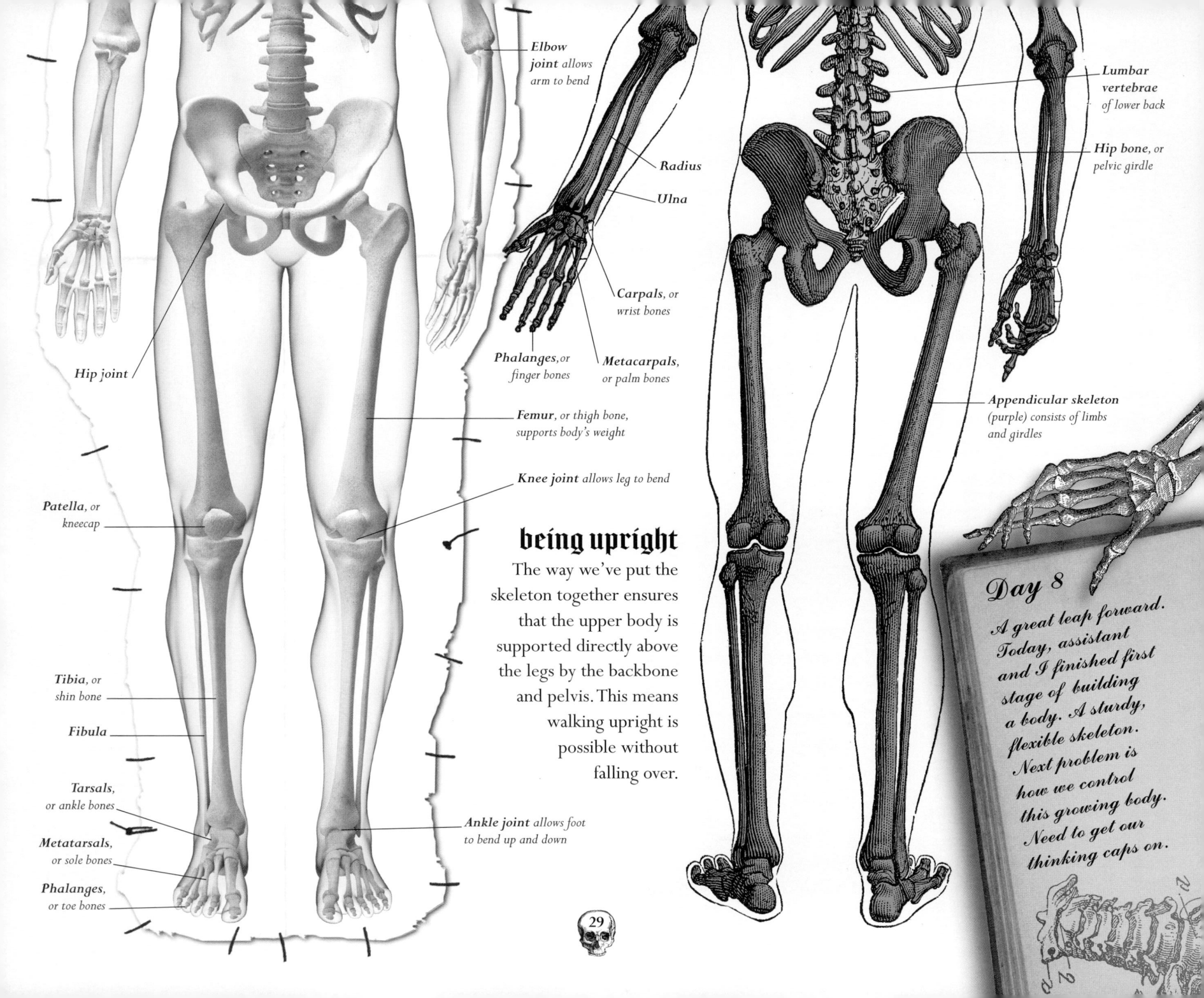

being upright

The way we've put the skeleton together ensures that the upper body is supported directly above the legs by the backbone and pelvis. This means walking upright is possible without falling over.

Cerebrum

Working as my assistant involves a great deal of observation, learning, remembering, and imagining. All those facilities are provided by the cerebrum, the key part of the brain. Its thin outer layer, the cortex, enables you to see, feel, think about, and respond to the world around you.

control center

Making up about 85 percent of the brain, the cerebrum is undoubtedly the brain's control center. It is divided into two halves, or hemispheres, each responsible for the opposite half of the body.

Premotor cortex *controls complex movements such as riding a bike*

Prefrontal cortex *is involved in thought, planning, and personality*

Broca's area *controls speech*

Deep groove *divides cerebrum into left and right hemispheres*

Right hemisphere *controls left-hand side of body and deals with art and music*

Left hemisphere *controls right-hand side of body and deals with language and math*

brain cells

You had better start counting because there are about 100 billion neurons, or nerve cells, in the cerebrum. Each one receives electrical signals from, and sends them to, thousands of other neurons through processes called dendrites and axons.

working areas

The cerebral cortex has certain areas that perform specific tasks: sensory areas receive messages from sensors in the skin and other places; motor areas send out instructions to muscles to move the body; and association areas analyze and interpret information.

Motor cortex *triggers muscles into movement*

Primary sensory cortex *enables you to feel touch and pain*

Sensory association cortex *interprets signals from skin receptors*

Wernicke's area *interprets the words you hear and see*

Visual association cortex *analyzes patterns of visual information to form images*

Primary visual cortex *interprets signals from the eyes about shapes, colors, and movement*

Primary auditory cortex *receives signals from the ears*

Auditory association cortex *analyzes and identifies sounds and their sources*

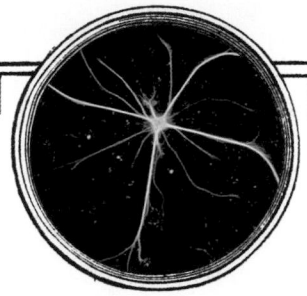

support staff

There are lots of neurons in the cerebrum, but there are 10 times as many support cells, such as this astrocyte. Support cells look after neurons and feed them. Some wrap themselves around the neurons to insulate and protect them.

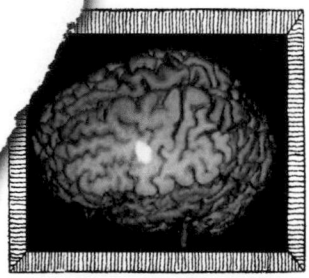

The motor cortex *"lights up" just before a person moves a finger.*

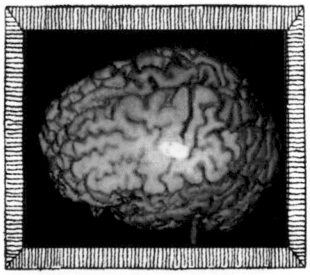

The sensory cortex *"lights up" as a person feels his or her finger moving.*

movement in action

Two MEG (magnetoencephalography) scans taken a fraction of a second apart (above) show the brain in action. They reveal which part of the cortex is active when its owner is doing or feeling something.

Central nervous system

Once installed, the brain needs to be linked up to the rest of the body. The first part of that process is to add the spinal cord. Together, the brain and spinal cord form the central nervous system, a command center that receives, analyzes, and stores incoming information and sends out instructions.

***Brain** is at the core of the central nervous system*

***Left and right hemispheres** separated to show "inner brain"*

***Inner view** of left hemisphere of cerebrum*

BACK

***Spinal cord** relays messages to and from the brain*

***Cerebellum** controls balance and helps coordinate movement*

***Brain stem** connects brain to spinal cord and automatically controls heart rate and breathing*

Spinal cord

in control

The central nervous system controls and coordinates most of what is going on inside the body, including the way you are turning the pages as you read this book.

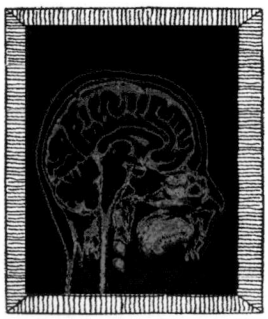

inner brain

The cerebrum dominates the brain landscape, so you need to get inside it to see what else is happening. If you slice through the corpus callosum—the mass of axon connections that links the two halves of the cerebral cortex—the hemispheres come apart.

limbic system

Made up of a "ring" of structures within the cerebrum, including the hippocampus and amygdala, the limbic system (right) controls emotions and plays a role in memory.

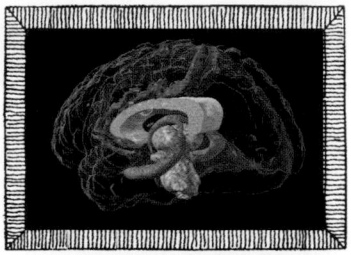

surround and protect

With the consistency of warm jelly, the brain can easily be damaged. It floats in a fluid, which cushions it from sudden jolts, and is surrounded by three layers of protective membranes and the skull (right).

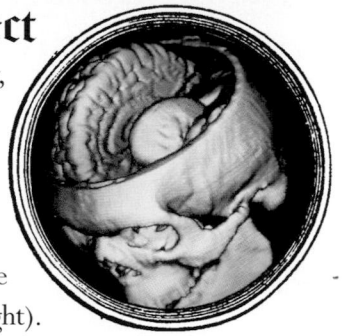

Corpus callosum *is a band of axons that connects the left and right hemispheres*

Thalamus *relays and filters messages going to cerebral cortex*

Hypothalamus *regulates many body activities including hunger, thirst, and sleep, and controls the pituitary gland*

FRONT

Pituitary gland *controls other hormone-releasing glands*

protective tunnel

The spinal cord runs down the back along a "tunnel" created by the bony arches of neighboring vertebrae in the backbone. This tunnel protects the spinal cord and its billions of neurons from damage.

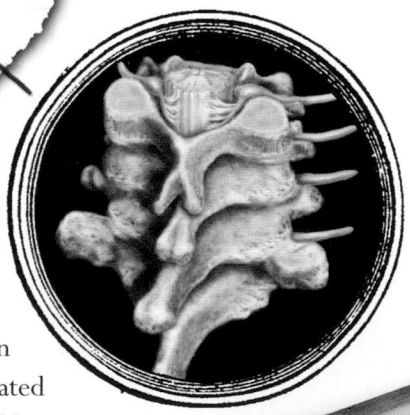

Spinal cord *seen in rear view*

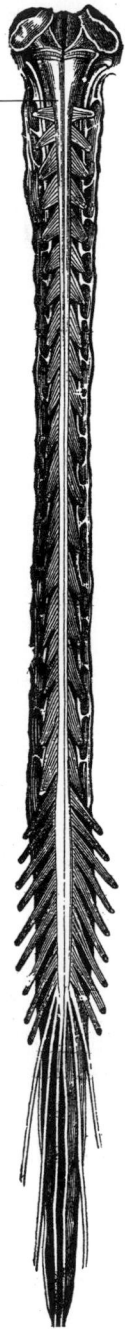

spinal cord

Starting at the base of the brain and running down most of the length of the backbone, the spinal cord relays information to and from the brain. But it also processes information. It controls many automatic reactions, called reflexes, such as automatically pulling your hand away from a hot object to keep from getting burned.

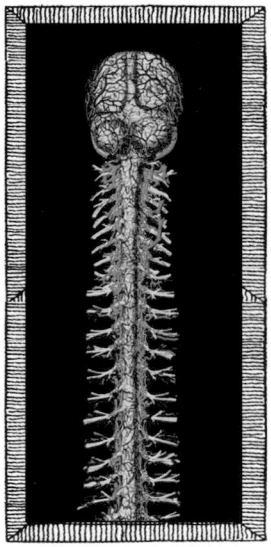

Brain and spinal cord *showing short spinal nerves.*

Day 9

Today, assistant and I used our gray matter to install a brain that thinks, feels, and tells its owner what to do. Added a spinal cord down the back. It's time to wire them up to the rest of the body.

Nerves

The next task is to hook up the brain and the spinal cord to the rest of the body, so the central nervous system can do its job. That's achieved through a massive network of cables, called nerves, that carry high-speed electrical signals to and from every nook and cranny of the body.

communication cables

Nerves are organized bundles of the long axons of neurons (nerve cells) that carry electrical signals to and from the central nervous system. There are 12 pairs of cranial nerves coming from the brain and brain stem, and 31 pairs of spinal nerves sprouting from the spinal cord.

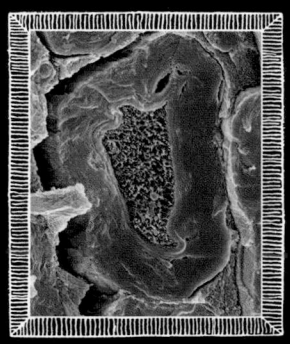

insulated axons

The axons (pink) inside this nerve bundle (brown) are each surrounded by a fatty sheath. This insulates them and increases the speed at which they transmit signals.

Cranial nerve *arising from brain*

Spinal nerve *arising from spinal cord*

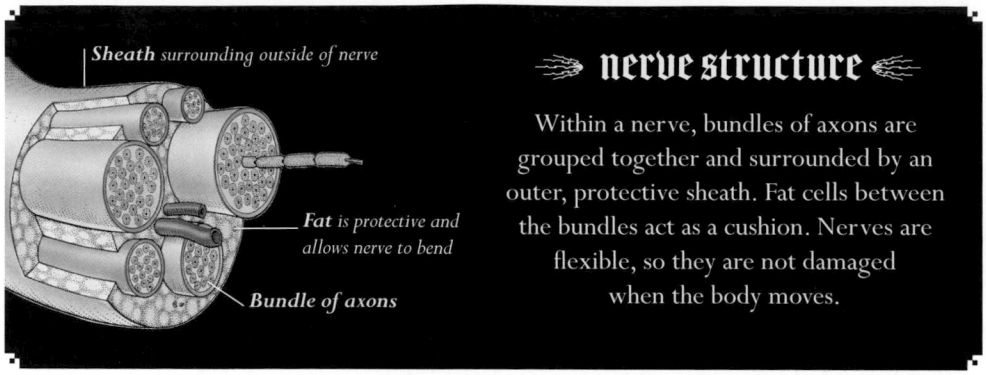

nerve structure

Within a nerve, bundles of axons are grouped together and surrounded by an outer, protective sheath. Fat cells between the bundles act as a cushion. Nerves are flexible, so they are not damaged when the body moves.

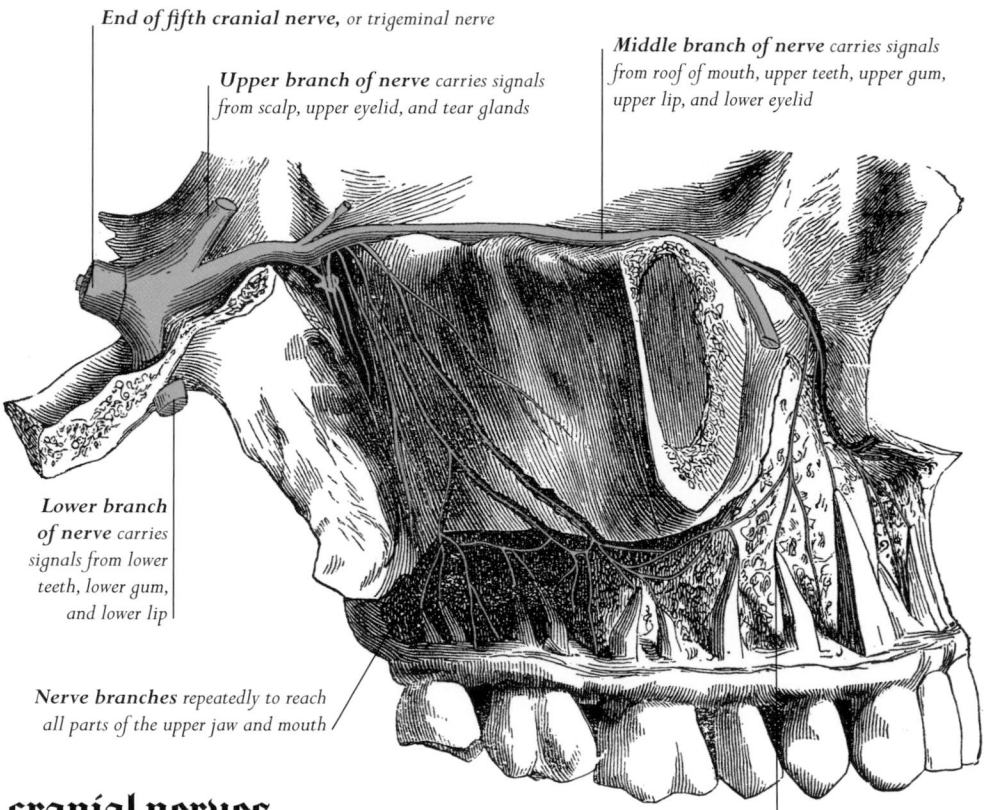

cranial nerves

Most cranial nerves supply the head and neck. Here you can see some of the branches of one of those nerves as it reaches out to parts of the face, mouth, and teeth. Ouch!

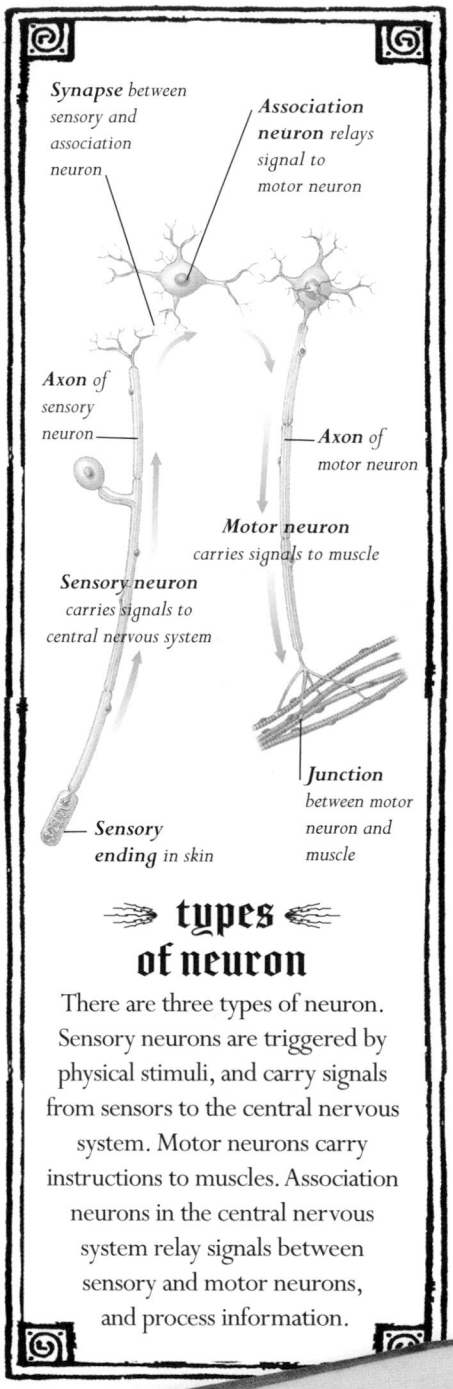

types of neuron

There are three types of neuron. Sensory neurons are triggered by physical stimuli, and carry signals from sensors to the central nervous system. Motor neurons carry instructions to muscles. Association neurons in the central nervous system relay signals between sensory and motor neurons, and process information.

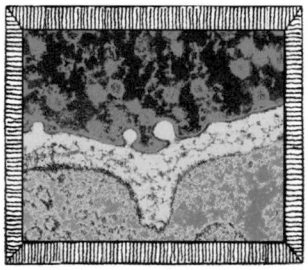

Gap (yellow) between ends of two neurons (blue and green)

synapse

A synapse is a junction between the ends of neurons where they are very close but do not touch. The neurons communicate with one another by sending chemical messengers across this synaptic gap.

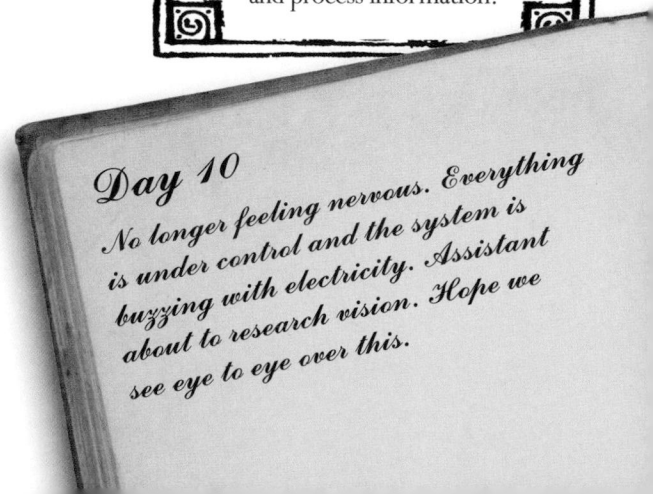

Eyes

Day 11
Assistant has seen the light. Now understands eye focus and can tell rods from cones. An excellent pupil. Next job—to keep an eye out for some ears.

The eyes are the body's most important sense organs. Whatever the conditions, automatic mechanisms ensure that the eye receives the right amount of light and focuses a sharp image on its light receptors. These send signals to the brain that enable you to see what is in front of you.

changing shape

The lens changes shape to form a sharp image on the retina whether we look at near or distant objects. A ring of ciliary muscle (yellow/orange) around the lens controls changes in lens shape.

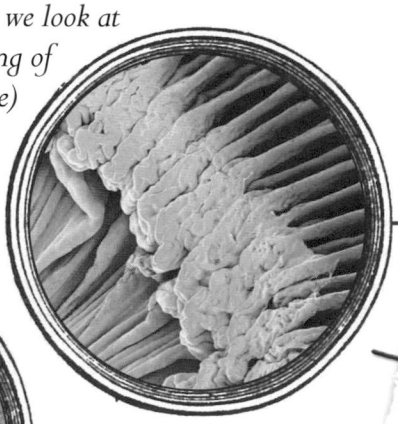

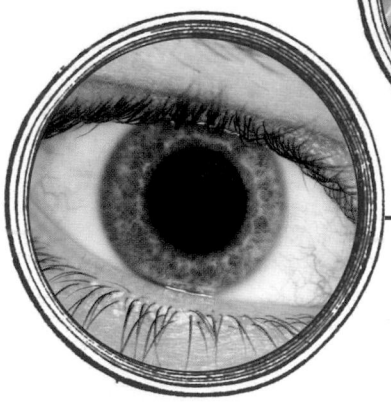

pupil control

Each pupil is a hole in the center of the colored iris through which light enters the back of the eye. By making the pupil smaller, the iris ensures that you're not dazzled by bright light. By making it bigger, the eye receives more light in darker conditions.

Pupil

***Iris** controls size of pupil*

***Eyelashes** protect eyes from dust and excess light*

***Lens** alters shape to focus light on the retina*

***Cornea** helps to focus light entering eye*

***Conjunctiva** is a thin, moist, protective membrane*

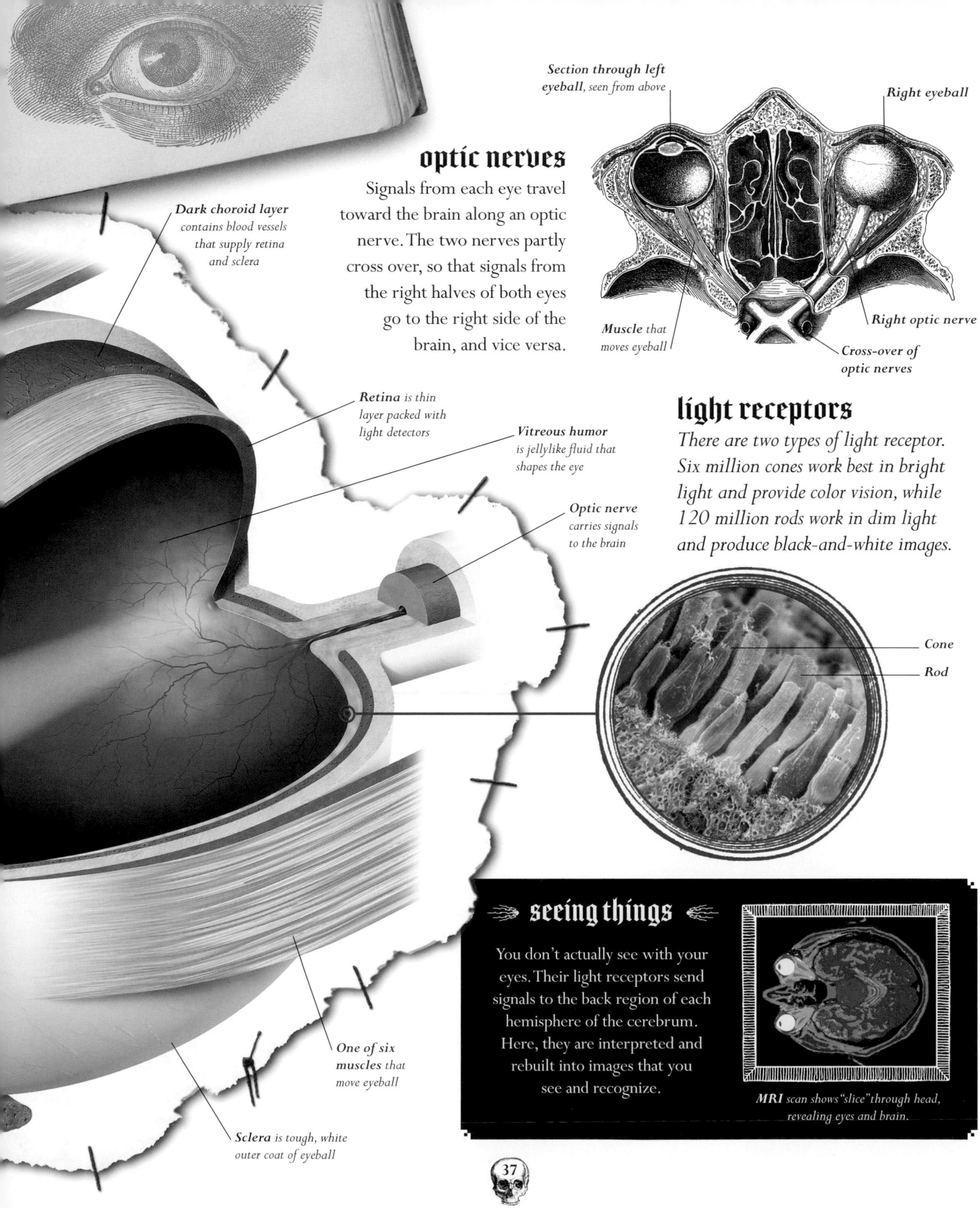

optic nerves

Signals from each eye travel toward the brain along an optic nerve. The two nerves partly cross over, so that signals from the right halves of both eyes go to the right side of the brain, and vice versa.

light receptors

There are two types of light receptor. Six million cones work best in bright light and provide color vision, while 120 million rods work in dim light and produce black-and-white images.

seeing things

You don't actually see with your eyes. Their light receptors send signals to the back region of each hemisphere of the cerebrum. Here, they are interpreted and rebuilt into images that you see and recognize.

***MRI** scan shows "slice" through head, revealing eyes and brain.*

Ears

Listen carefully, because it's time to assemble the ears. Most of the ear is protected inside the temporal bone of the skull. It's here that sound waves traveling through the air are detected.

inside the ear

Look inside the ear and you'll discover three zones. The outer part is the ear canal. The air-filled middle section has the eardrum at one end and the oval window at the other. The fluid-filled inner section has the cochlea and balance sensors.

Temporal bone of the skull

Ear flap directs sound waves into the ear canal

outer canal

Sounds are created when objects vibrate and produce pressure waves in the air. These sound waves enter the ear canal. Earwax (right) is produced to clean the canal and to deter insects.

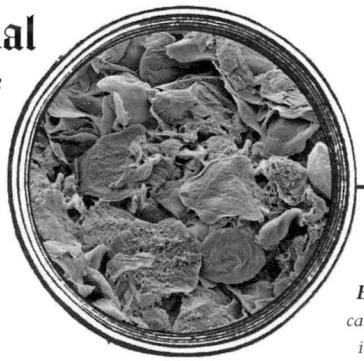

Ear canal carries sound into the ear

ossicles

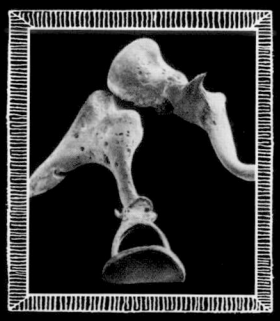

The three ear bones, or ossicles, are the smallest bones in the body. The tiniest, the stirrup, is no bigger than a grain of rice. The others are called the hammer and the anvil.

transmit and amplify

The ossicles transmit vibrations from the eardrum to the oval window. When the eardrum vibrates, the bones move the oval window, sending vibrations through fluid in the inner ear. This action also amplifies the sound.

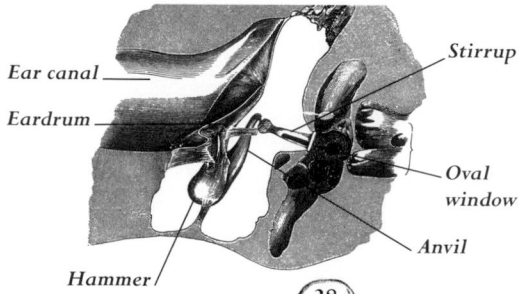

ear drum

When sound waves hit the eardrum (left, red) it vibrates. These vibrations are passed to the ossicles. The hammer (orange) is attached to the eardrum.

***Semicircular canals** detect head movements and aid balance*

***Ossicles**, or ear bones*

***Oval window** is entrance to fluid-filled inner ear*

***Cochlea** contains the receptors that detect sound waves*

***Eardrum** is taut membrane at the end of the ear canal*

***Eustachian tube** keeps air pressure inside ear equal to the air pressure outside*

***Tiny "hairs"** attached to sound-detecting hair cells*

cochlea

The snail-shell-shaped cochlea contains receptors called hair cells that detect vibrations passing through its fluid. These vibrations bend the "hairs" on top of the cells, causing them to send signals to the brain. The brain interprets these signals as sounds.

***Section through cochlea** to show its canals*

***Auditory nerve** carries signals to the brain*

***Position** of hair cells*

in balance

Parts of the inner ear send signals to the brain to help you balance. Three semicircular canals sense head movements. The utricle and saccule contain hair cells with crystals (below, blue) on the end. They sense your head's angle by the way the crystals hang on the hairs.

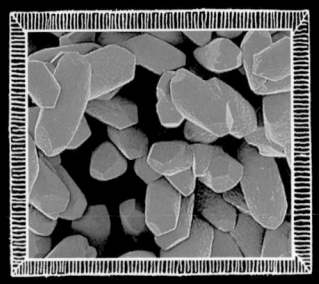

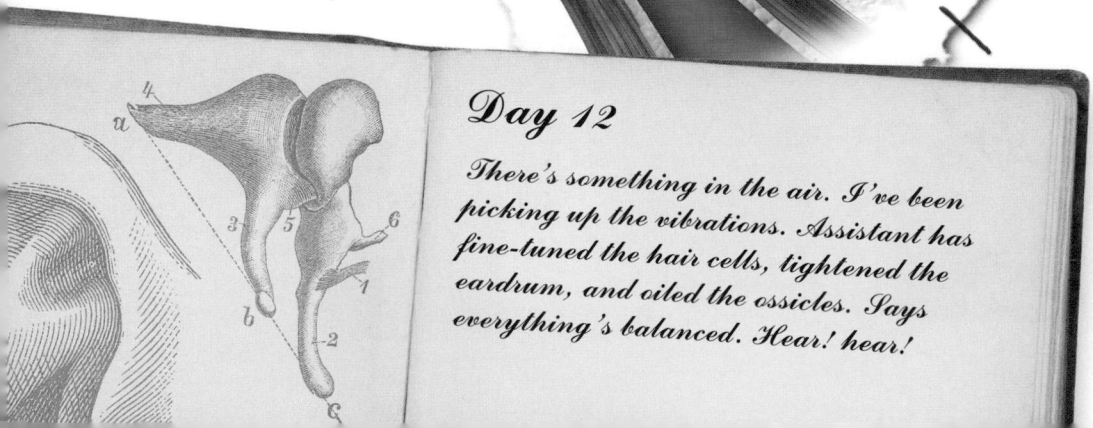

Control systems

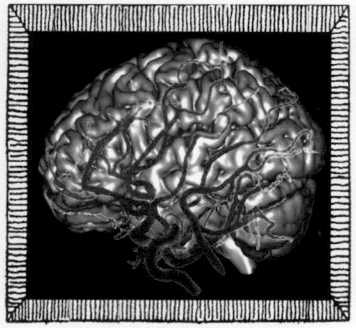

Without some form of control, body processes would go their own way at their own pace. There would be chaos. Fortunately, the two control systems we've installed keep things in order. The nervous system uses high-speed electrical signals for immediate effect. The endocrine system releases chemicals that work more slowly.

busy brain

This special X-ray (above) shows the mass of blood vessels that supply the brain with blood. They are needed because the busy brain consumes one-fifth of the body's oxygen and glucose, even though it makes up just 2 percent of the body's weight.

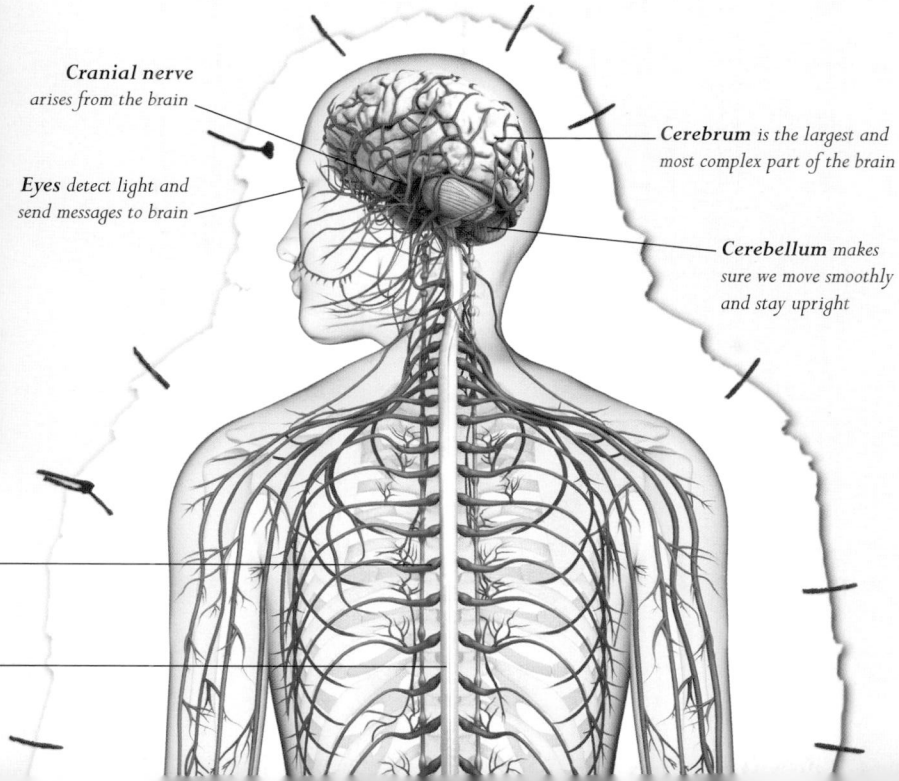

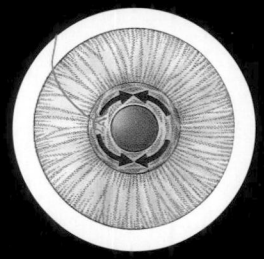

Circular muscles *make pupil smaller.*

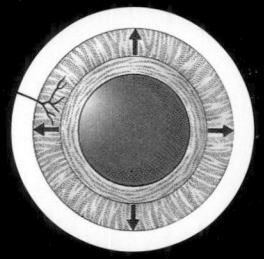

Radial muscles *make pupil larger.*

autonomic nervous system

You probably didn't know about this "hidden" branch of the nervous system, but you'd be lost without it. It carries instructions to internal organs and regulates what they do. For example, it controls the muscles that make the pupil wider or narrower.

nervous system

Billions of neurons, thousands of miles of nerves, and the huge processing power of the brain and spinal cord—we've assembled them all together to create a nervous system that's constantly buzzing with electrical signals.

Median nerve *serves the forearm and fingers*

Nerve plexus *is where nerves merge and separate*

Sciatic nerve *serves thigh, lower leg, and foot*

Tibial nerve *serves calf and sole of foot*

awake or asleep

A good night's sleep is what the brain needs to sort out events from the previous day. But during this downtime it doesn't switch off, especially during dreaming. In these scans (below), the red areas are the most active.

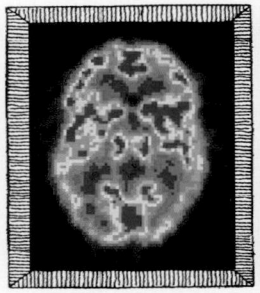

PET scan *of brain during dreaming sleep.*

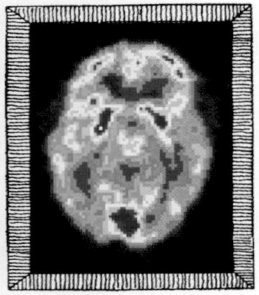

PET scan *of awake but resting brain.*

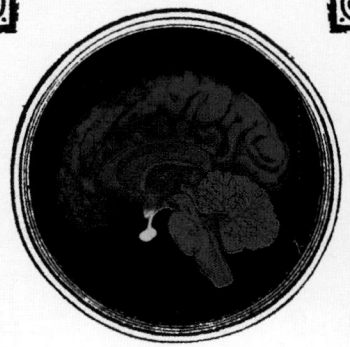

pituitary gland

Sticking out from the base of the brain, the pea-sized pituitary gland (above, orange) is a powerful player in another control system, the endocrine system. The pituitary gland and other glands release hormones to regulate processes such as growth.

Day 13

Nervous network in place and pituitary gland switched on. Assistant questioned whether brain is still busy when we sleep. What nerve! Time to plumb in the blood supply.

Blood vessels

Now that the bones are in place, we need to lay down the body's supply system. This consists of a vast network of blood vessels called arteries, veins, and capillaries that, stretched out, would wrap around the Earth four times. Blood vessels carry blood that delivers essential supplies to the body's cells.

living tubes

Blood vessels are "living tubes" because they are made from living cells. They vary in size from the biggest arteries and veins, which are the width of your thumb, to tiny capillaries, which you'll need a microscope to see. Let's compare arteries and veins.

Basilic vein *carries blood from the hand and arm*

Brachial artery *supplies blood to the upper arm*

arteries

Carrying oxygen-rich blood from the heart to the tissues, arteries have thick walls with layers of muscular and elastic tissues. The walls expand and recoil—you can feel this as a "pulse"—every time blood is pumped through them by the heart.

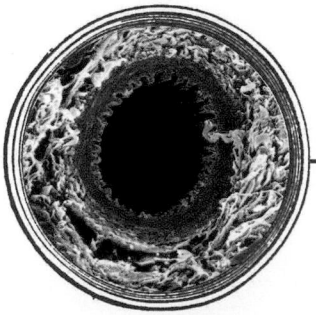

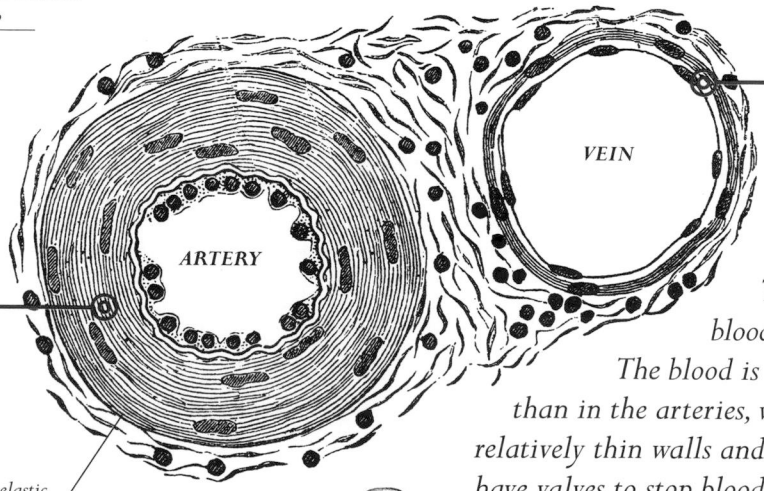

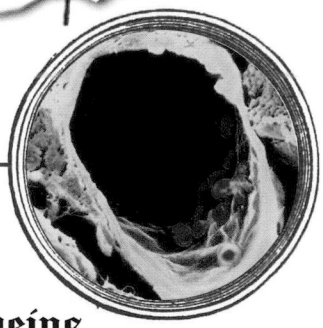

veins

These vessels carry oxygen-poor blood from the tissues to the heart. The blood is under much lower pressure than in the arteries, which is why veins have relatively thin walls and a bigger central space. Veins have valves to stop blood from flowing "backward."

Thick muscle *and elastic layers in the wall of the artery*

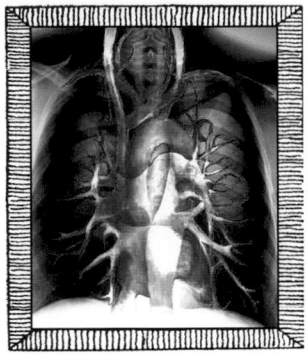

viewing vessels

This image (left) shows blood vessels inside the chest of a person. It's produced using a technique called MRA (magnetic resonance angiography). The big arching vessel in the middle is the aorta, the artery that carries oxygen-rich blood from the heart.

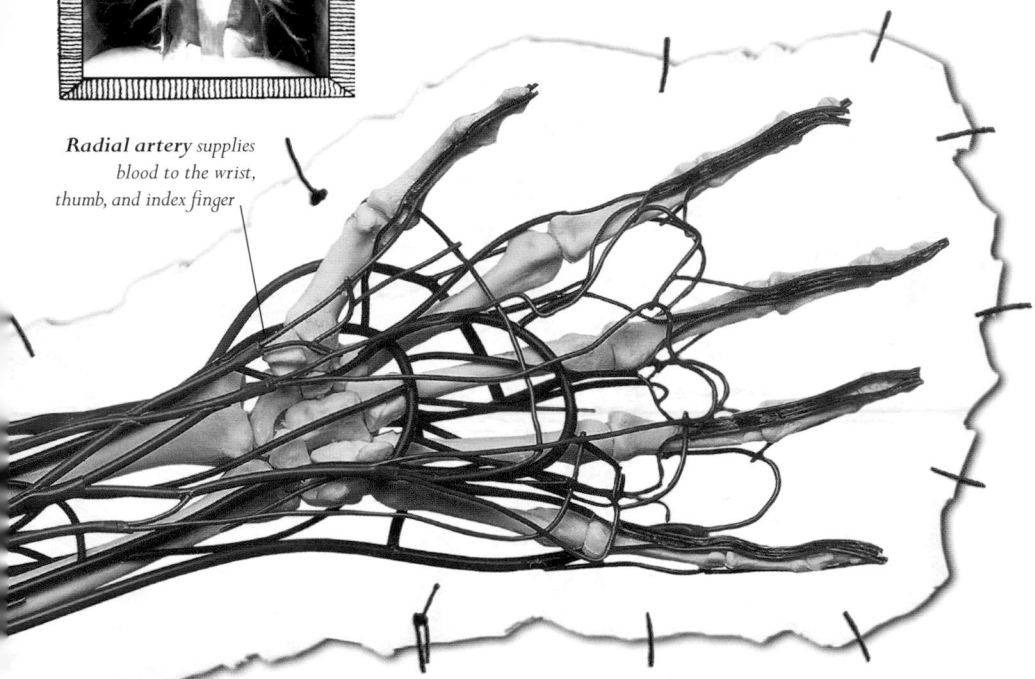

cell supplies

This is a unique view of the capillary network. As cells are never far from one of these tiny capillaries, there's no danger of them going short of essential supplies, such as food and oxygen, or being unable to get rid of unwanted waste.

capillary link

Capillaries may be microscopic, but they make up an amazing 98 percent of the total length of the blood vessel network. They arise from the narrowest artery branches, and carry blood through the tissues before merging to form the smallest vein branches. That means they link arteries to veins. That's some feat of plumbing!

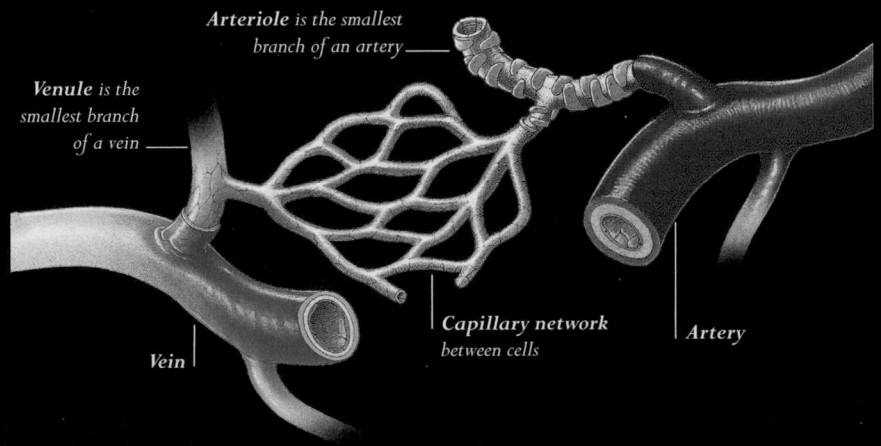

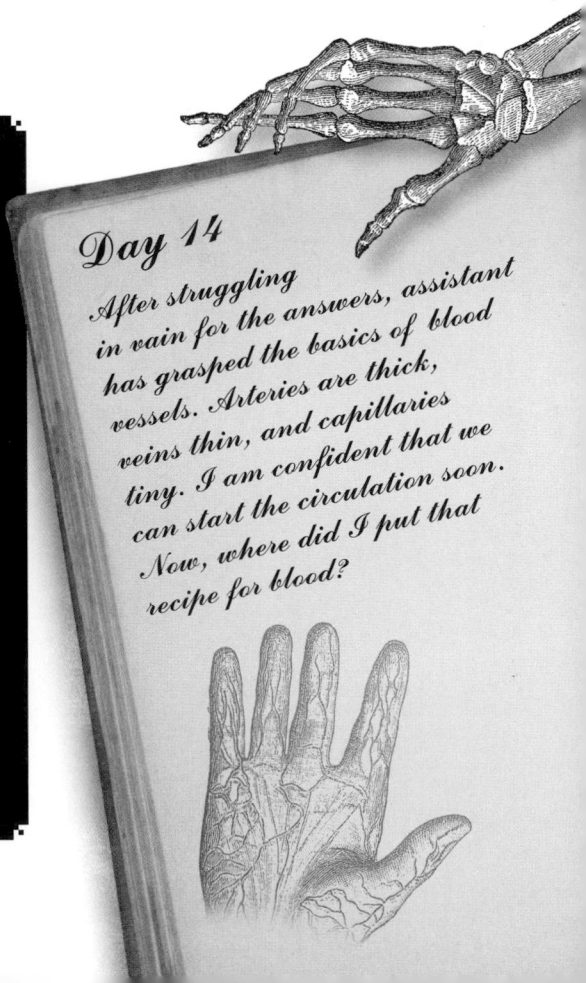

Blood

Now the blood vessels are in place, they can be filled. Ten pints (five liters) of blood flow around the body, delivering oxygen, food, and other essentials to cells, as well as removing waste material. Blood also fights infection by destroying disease-causing microorganisms called pathogens.

hemoglobin

Blood cells are red because they're packed with an orange-red-colored protein called hemoglobin. Each molecule of this special substance can pick up four oxygen molecules in the lungs and deliver them to the body's cells. With 250 million hemoglobin molecules inside one red blood cell, that's one billion oxygen molecules carried per cell. And with 25 trillion red blood cells traveling around your body, that's... well, you do the math.

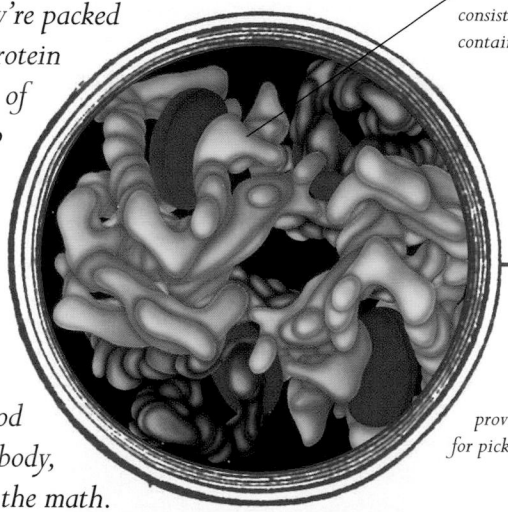

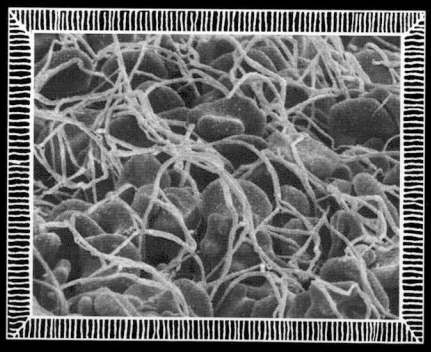

A net of fibrin threads *traps red and other blood cells to make a blood clot.*

repair kit

If a blood vessel is damaged, by a cut in the skin, for example, a self-repair mechanism automatically halts blood loss. First, platelets stick to each other in order to temporarily plug the leak. Then they trigger the conversion of a dissolved blood protein into fibers that create a blood clot to seal the wound.

red blood cells

Unlike other body cells, oxygen-carrying red blood cells lack a nucleus, and are instead packed with hemoglobin molecules. Red blood cells live for about 120 days. They are produced at the rate of two million per second by red bone marrow. Small and bendy, red blood cells squeeze through the narrowest capillaries to pick up oxygen or to deliver it to tissue cells.

Neutrophils *track down pathogens and eat them*

Platelets *are cell fragments, not whole cells*

white blood cells

Unlike their more numerous red partners, white blood cells come in several varieties. They have a nucleus and are able to squeeze through the walls of capillaries to enter tissues. Neutrophils and monocytes eat pathogens, while lymphocytes use chemical warfare to destroy their prey.

blood composition

You can see the composition of blood by spinning a sample in a machine called a centrifuge. Watery plasma, which transports dissolved food, waste, hormones, and other substances, makes up 55 percent, red blood cells 44 percent, and white blood cells and platelets 1 percent.

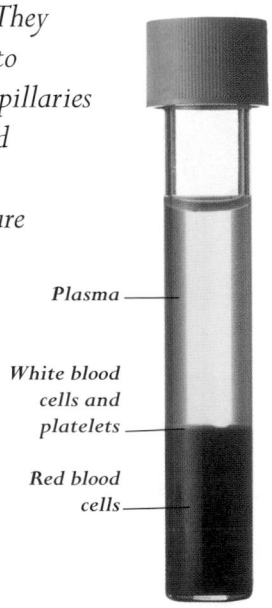

Heart

Let's get to the heart of the matter. Working tirelessly to push blood around the body, the heart has separated left and right sides, each with two chambers. Both sides contract together about once a second, the right side pumping blood to the lungs, the left pumping blood to the body.

coronary supply

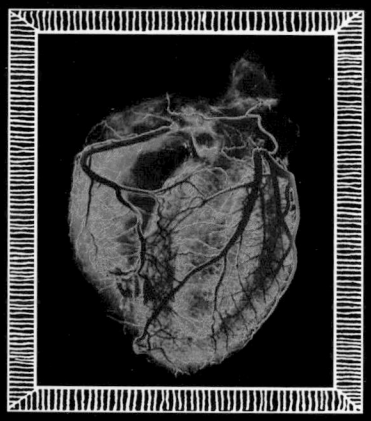

The blood rushing through the heart cannot supply the heart's muscle cells with fuel and oxygen. A separate blood supply is provided by the coronary arteries that arise from the aorta and branch throughout the heart wall.

one way

Two sets of valves guarantee a one-way flow of blood through the heart. Without these valves, blood would flow in two directions and would not circulate around the body. Each valve has flaps that open to allow blood through, and close to stop it from flowing backward.

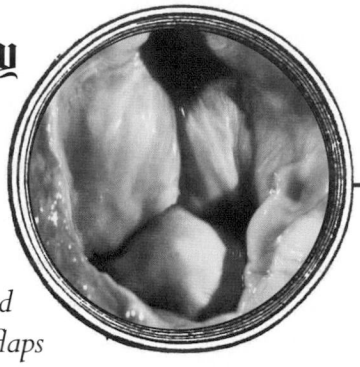

heartstrings

Known as heartstrings, these tough cords connect the flaps of the bicuspid and tricuspid valves to the ventricle walls. When the ventricles contract, the heartstrings stop the valves from turning inside out like an umbrella in a gale.

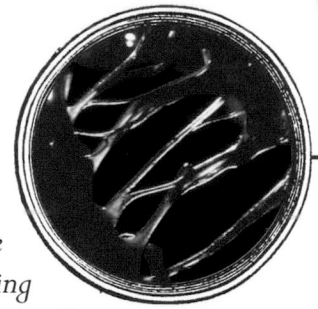

Superior vena cava *carries oxygen-poor blood from the upper body to the right atrium*

Right atrium *receives oxygen-poor blood from the body and houses the heart's "pacemaker"*

Inferior vena cava *carries oxygen-poor blood from the lower body to the right atrium*

semilunar valves

Each semilunar valve has three pocketlike flaps that flatten as blood rushes between them during contraction. They fill up and block the exit to prevent blood from flowing backward during relaxation.

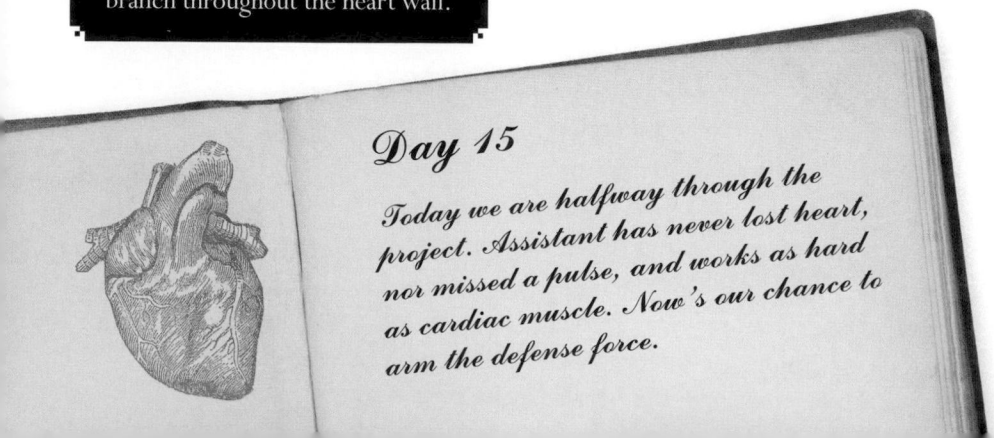

Aorta *carries oxygen-rich blood to the body*

Pulmonary artery *carries oxygen-poor blood to the lungs*

Semilunar valves *guard exits from ventricles*

Pulmonary veins *carry oxygen-rich blood from the lungs to the heart*

Left atrium *receives oxygen-rich blood from the lungs*

Left ventricle *has thicker wall needed to pump blood to the body*

Tricuspid valve *between right atrium and right ventricle (bicuspid valve on left side)*

Right ventricle *pumps blood to the lungs*

heartbeat

Each heartbeat is not a single, big contraction but a precisely timed sequence of three stages. These ensure that, together, the left and right sides of the heart fill with blood, then contract to force blood out of the heart.

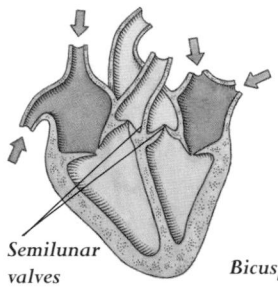

1. The heart is relaxing. Oxygen-rich blood (red) from the lungs and oxygen-poor blood (blue) from the body enter the left and right atria, respectively. Semilunar valves are closed.

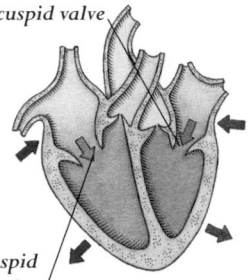

2. Left and right atria contract together to push blood through the open bicuspid and tricuspid valves, into the ventricles. The semilunar valves remain closed.

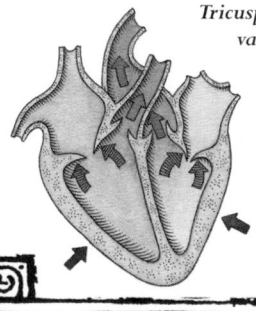

3. As the two ventricles contract together to pump blood along the aorta and pulmonary artery, the bicuspid and tricuspid valves close, while the semilunar valves open.

heart muscle

The cardiac muscle fibers, or cells, that make up the heart's wall form a close-knit network. Under the control of the heart's "pacemaker," the muscle fibers contract without tiring, and without a break, for a whole lifetime.

Lymph vessels and nodes

As the circulatory system performs its delivery service to cells, it leaves behind fluid in the tissues. We need to install a system of tubes to drain excess fluid, now called lymph, and return it to the blood. On the way, defense cells will destroy disease-causing pathogens in the lymph.

lymph nodes

Like beads on a string, these bean-shaped swellings occur along lymph vessels. Lymph nodes contain immune system cells—macrophages, which trap and engulf debris and bacteria, and lymphocytes, which disable or destroy specific enemies.

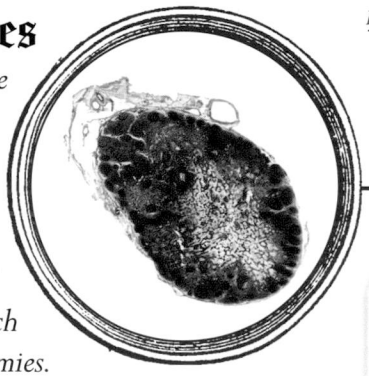

one-way vessels

Lymph vessels are blind-ending and carry lymph in one direction. They have no "pump" to push lymph through them. Instead they're squeezed by skeletal muscles and equipped with valves to prevent backflow.

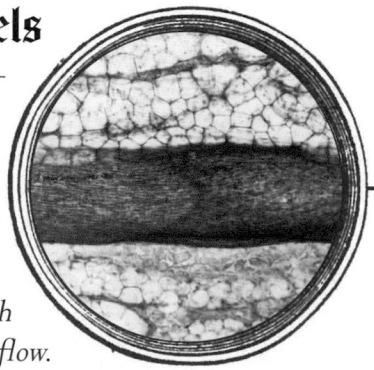

***Lymph node** processes lymph flowing through it*

***Thoracic duct** is a major lymphatic vessel*

chemical warfare

Two groups of lymphocytes—B cells and T cells—are the lynchpins of the immune system. Each type of cell works in a different way, but both attack specific pathogens and retain a "memory" of them should they return to attack the body again.

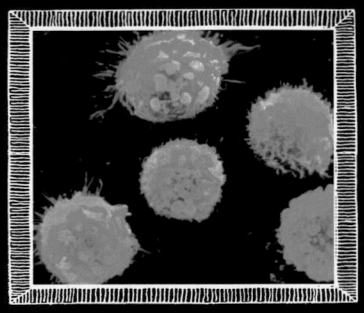

B cells *release antibodies that target and disable specific pathogens.*

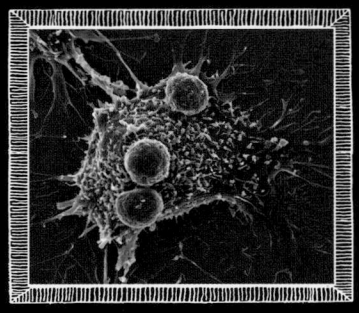

T cells *can destroy a cancer cell by punching holes in its cell membrane.*

Lymph vessel *carries lymph toward major lymph ducts*

Lymph *from thoracic duct empties into left subclavian vein*

draining tissues

Working alongside the circulatory system, lymph vessels extend to all parts of the body. Unlike arteries and veins, however, they end blindly. The smallest branches, lymph capillaries, drain surplus fluid, now called lymph, from the tissues, then merge to form larger lymph vessels. These, in turn, empty into two ducts that pour lymph into the subclavian veins.

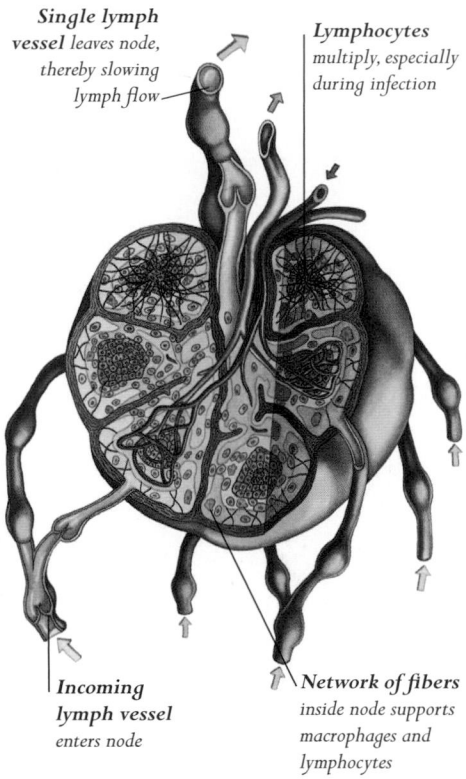

inside a node

The interior of a lymph node is crisscrossed with fibers that support macrophages and lymphocytes. The fibers slow the flow of lymph as macrophages pick off any intruders. When lymphocytes identify specific pathogens, they multiply rapidly. They either attack directly, or release antibodies to disable pathogens for macrophages to attack.

pathogen eaters

You've already come across white blood cells called monocytes. Once these cells leave the bloodstream and move into lymph nodes or infected tissues, they become big, hungry, pathogen-eating macrophages. This macrophage (right, gold) is rounding up some bacteria (red).

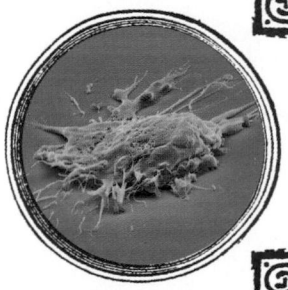

Transportation systems

Once the body is complete, its trillions of cells will demand first-class transportation systems. The circulatory system delivers essential materials to every cell and removes waste products. The lymphatic system drains excess fluid from the tissues and helps the circulatory system to defend the body against pathogens.

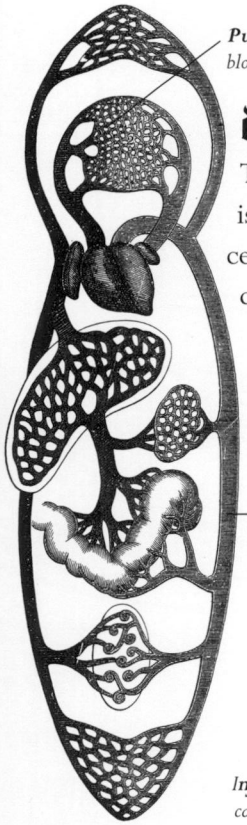

double circulation

Time for you to discover how blood is pumped along to linked "loops" centered on the heart. One loop carries blood to the lungs to pick up oxygen. The other loop carries blood to the body's tissues to give up oxygen.

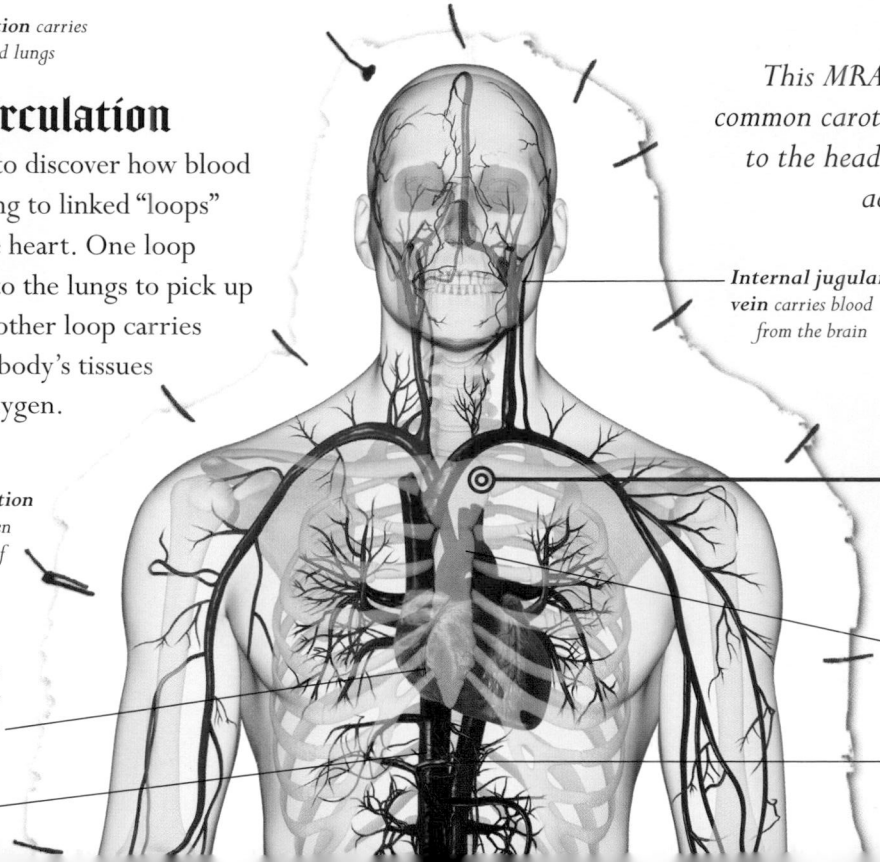

taken to the top

This MRA image (below) shows the left and right common carotid arteries that carry blood up the neck to the head. At the bottom, you can see the curving aortic arch from which the arteries arise.

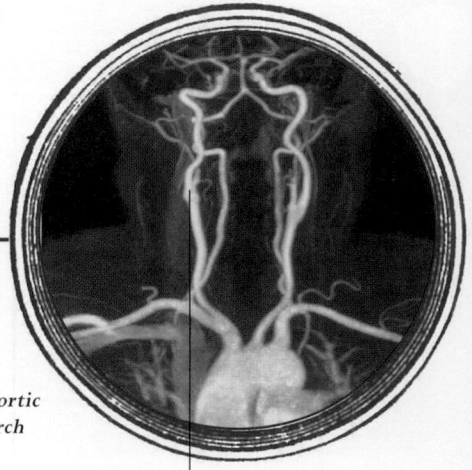

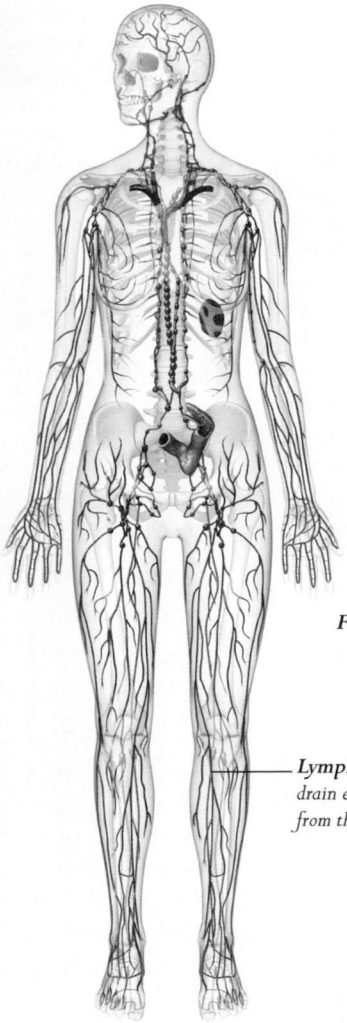

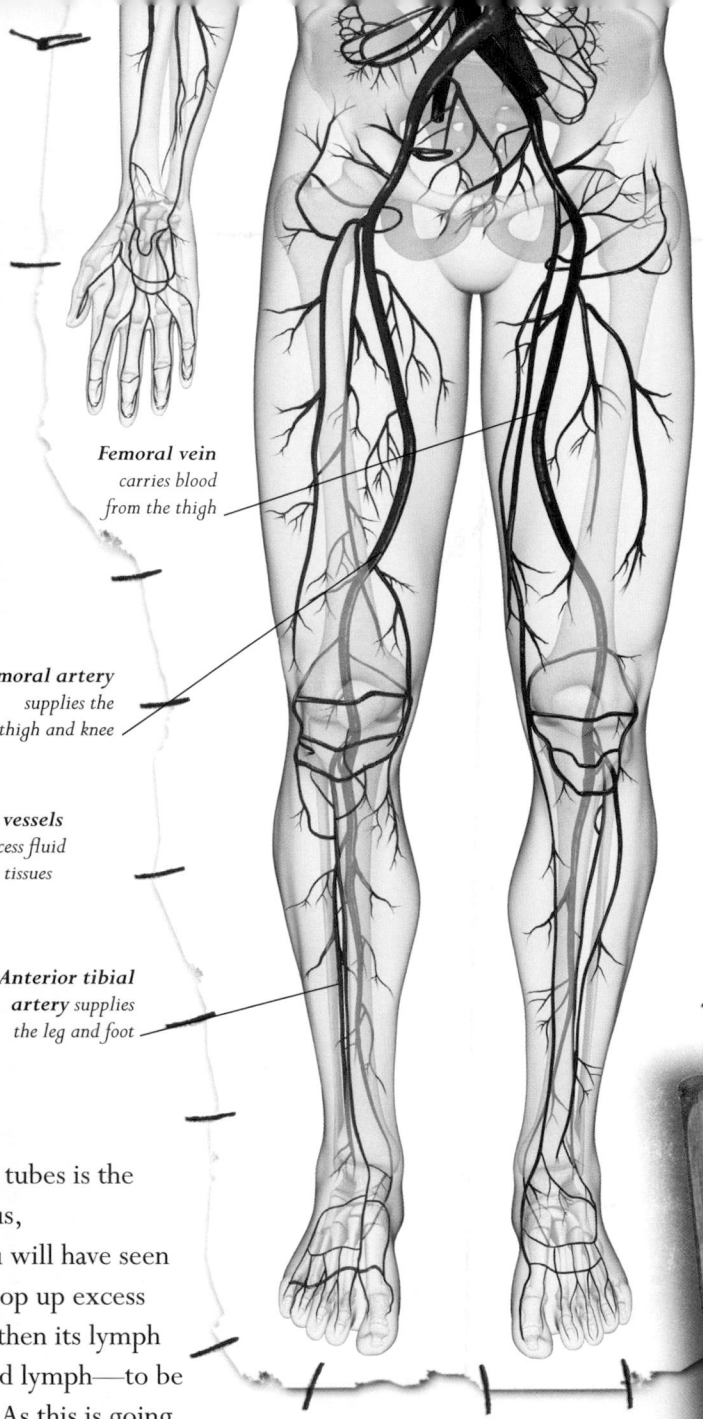

circulatory system

Put together the heart, blood vessels, and blood and you get the circulatory or cardiovascular system. You can see the major veins in blue and the major arteries in red. The exceptions are the pulmonary artery (which carries oxygen-poor blood) and the pulmonary vein (which carries oxygen-rich blood).

changing color

Although we've color-coded blood vessels red or blue to show whether or not they are carrying oxygen-rich blood, they aren't really that color, nor is the blood inside them. But blood does change color as it travels around the body. Oxygen-rich blood is bright red (far right), while oxygen-poor blood is a darker purple-red.

lymphatic system

This network of blind-ending tubes is the body's second, and less famous, transportation system. As you will have seen already, its tiny capillaries scoop up excess fluid from the body's tissues, then its lymph vessels carry that fluid—called lymph—to be returned to the bloodstream. As this is going on, lymph flows through lymph nodes that filter out debris and pathogens.

Day 16

Transportation systems have proved tricky. Assistant did something wrong and it made my blood boil. Never mind, the job's done now, and assistant is ready for a course in waste disposal.

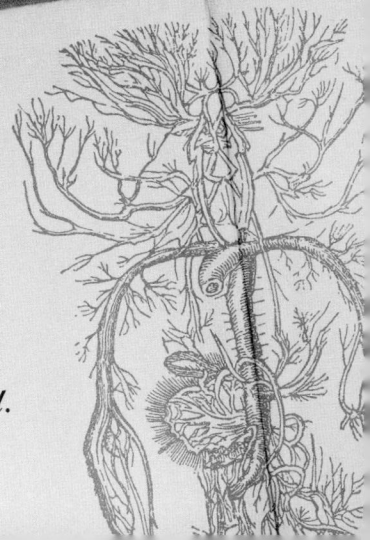

Kidneys

It's important that the composition of blood circulating around the body is kept constant so cells live in stable conditions. We need to add two blood-filtering kidneys at the back of the abdomen. The kidneys remove poisonous waste and excess water, which they combine to make urine. This is later released from the body through the ureter.

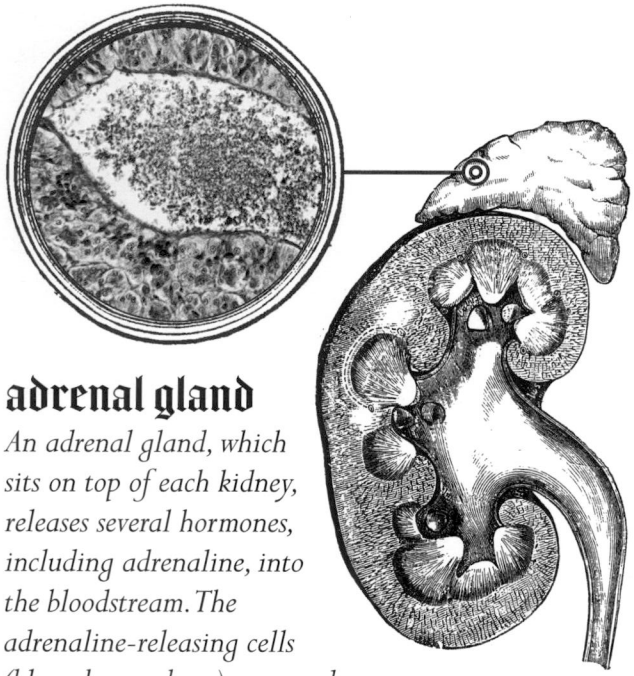

adrenal gland

An adrenal gland, which sits on top of each kidney, releases several hormones, including adrenaline, into the bloodstream. The adrenaline-releasing cells (blue, shown above) surround a vein. If the body is under threat, adrenaline works with the nervous system to help combat stress.

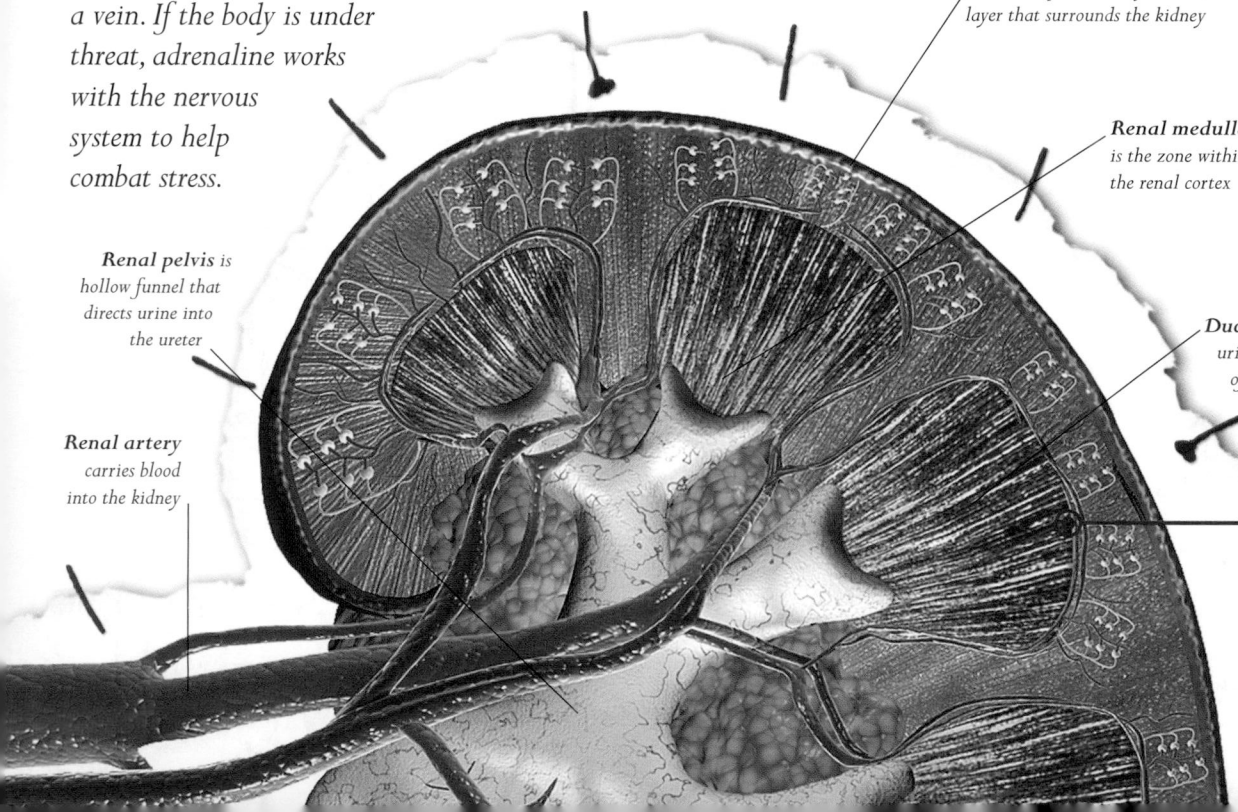

filtration units

Each of the million nephrons in a kidney consists of a cluster of capillaries, called a glomerulus (below, pink), and a coiled tubule. Liquid filtered from the glomerulus is processed as it passes along the tubule, returning "useful" substances to the blood and leaving urine to flow into the pelvis.

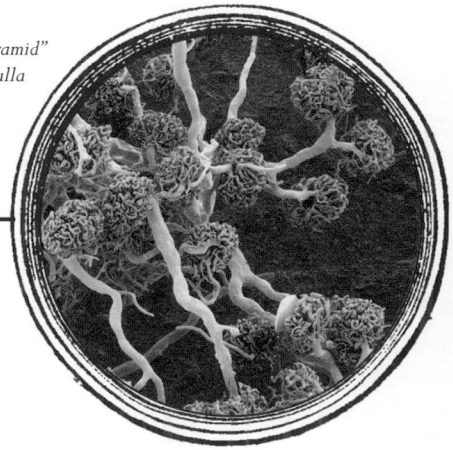

Renal vein
carries blood away

Renal cortex
forms the outer portion of the kidney

Ureter
carries urine from the kidney

blood supply

The two kidneys (shown in the angiogram, below) receive one-quarter of the heart's output of blood. That's the daily equivalent of 12 bathtubs full of blood, from which just ½ gallon (1.5 liters) of urine is produced.

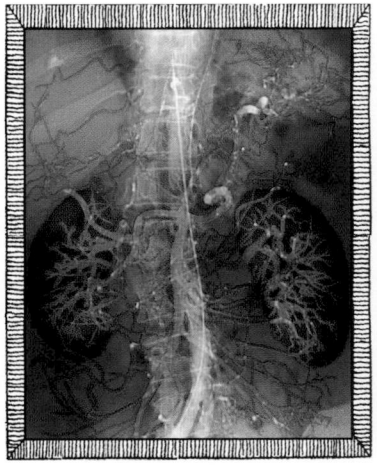

urine producer

Look inside a kidney and its structure is clear to see. There is a cortex surrounding the "pyramids" of the medulla that lead to the hollow pelvis. Nephrons in the outer cortex and medulla filter blood to make urine. This flows down collecting ducts to the pelvis, and on to the ureter.

kidney transplant

This is a living kidney, taken from one person (the donor) and about to be moved or transplanted into the body of another person (the recipient) who needs it. The donated kidney will take over the functions of the recipient's kidneys, which have stopped working due to damage or disease.

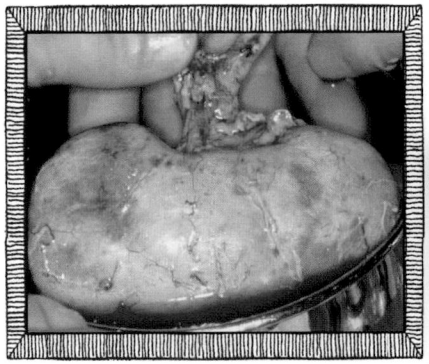

Urinary system

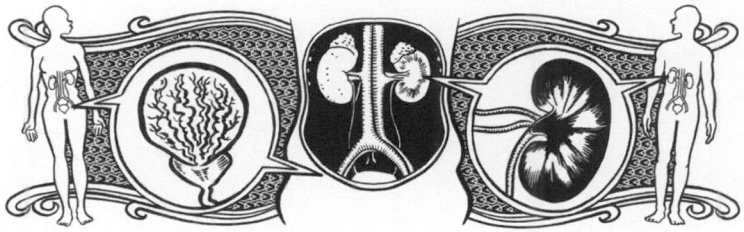

Day 18

Am feeling the urge to congratulate assistant. All tubes plumbed in correctly, the bladder working at full stretch, and urine flowing freely. Now must chew over the subject of food and eating. Talking of which, I wonder what's for dinner? Not kidneys, I hope.

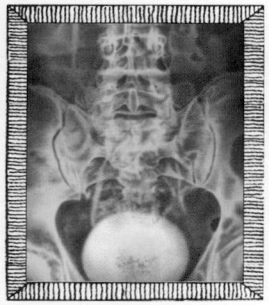

Filling

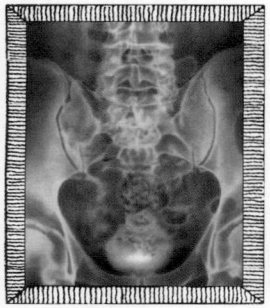

Emptying

Working day and night, your kidneys release a constant trickle of urine. Without some means of storing urine, life would be very unpleasant. That's why we've added other parts of the urinary system. Urine is delivered by two ureters to a very stretchy, muscular bag called the bladder. This stores urine until you feel the need to release it through the urethra.

fill and empty

You can see in these special X-rays a bladder (above, green) filling and emptying. As the bladder fills, receptors in its stretched wall send messages to your brain, so you feel the urge to urinate.

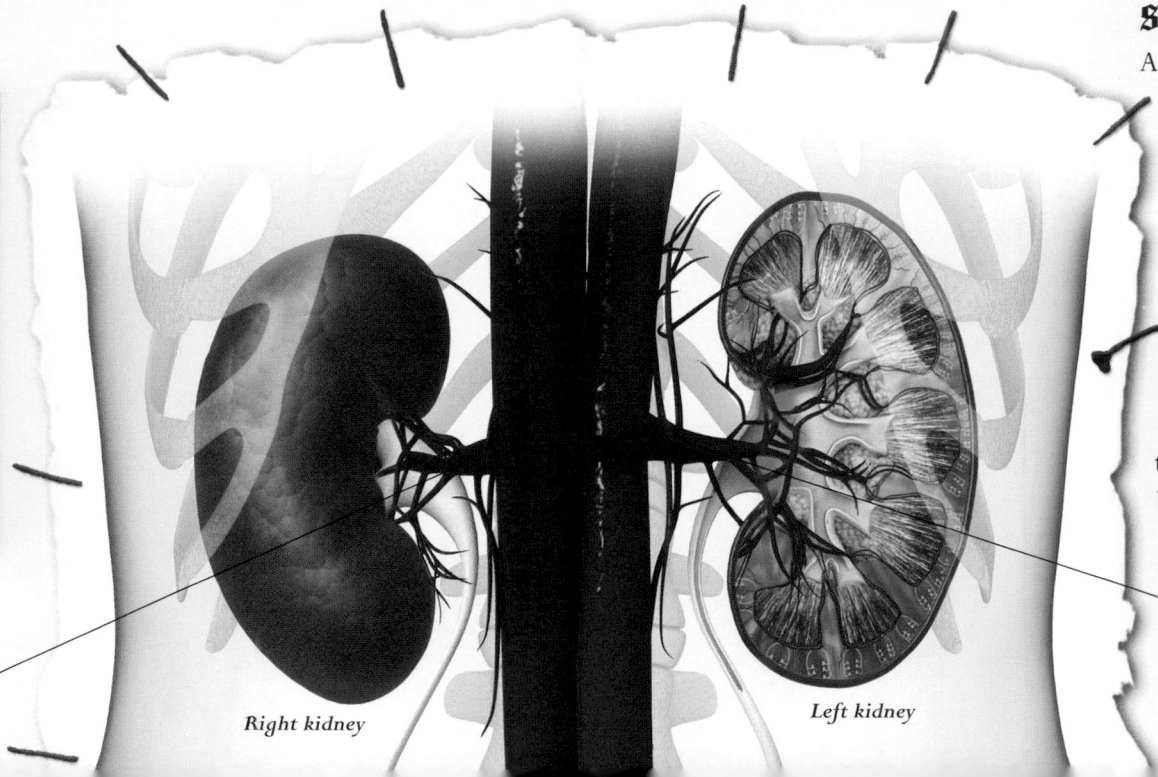

store and release

As the bladder fills with urine, a ring of muscle called a sphincter contracts to close its exit and stop leakage. When the bladder is full, and you feel the need to urinate, you relax the sphincter. The bladder wall contracts rhythmically to push urine out of the body through the urethra.

Inferior vena cava *carries oxygen-poor blood toward heart*

Right ureter *carries urine from right kidney to bladder*

Aorta *carries oxygen-rich blood from heart*

Bladder *stores urine until it is released*

ureter

Urine is transported from kidney to bladder by a ureter, which plays an active role in the process. In this section of a ureter (above) you can see layers of smooth muscle (darker red). Muscular contractions pass down the ureter, pushing urine through an opening in the back wall of the bladder.

bladder wall

The stretchy wall of the bladder consists mainly of smooth muscle (above). This type of muscle works automatically without you noticing it, and contracts slowly and smoothly. You'll come across it in other organs, too, including the ureters.

Urethra *carries urine from the bladder to the outside of the body*

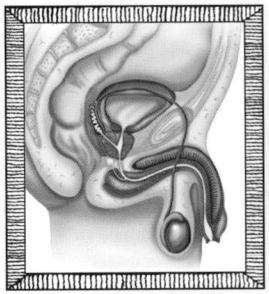

Male reproductive system

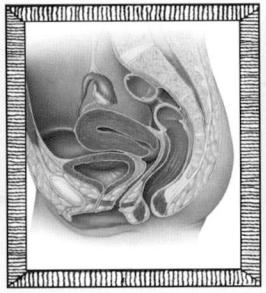

Female reproductive system

reproductive system

Located in the same part of the body as the urinary system, male and female reproductive systems differ in structure, but both are involved in producing special cells that join up to make babies.

Teeth

Now we must provide our body-in-progress with the tools it needs to feed. Unlike snakes, humans can't swallow big chunks of food whole. That's why we need to install a set of teeth—ideal for chopping and crushing food into tiny pieces.

tooth types

The versatile dental toolkit consists of chisel-shaped incisors, pointed canines, and premolars and molars, both with ridges called cusps for chewing.

Canines *grip, pierce, and tear food*

Premolars *aid molars in chewing food*

Molars *crush and grind food*

enamel

The hardest material in the body is white enamel. It must withstand the pressure, and wear and tear, of regular biting and chewing. Enamel doesn't contain cells or blood vessels so it cannot repair itself if it gets damaged.

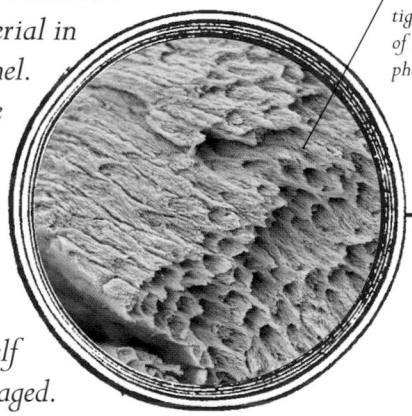

Enamel *consists of tightly packed rods of hard calcium phosphate*

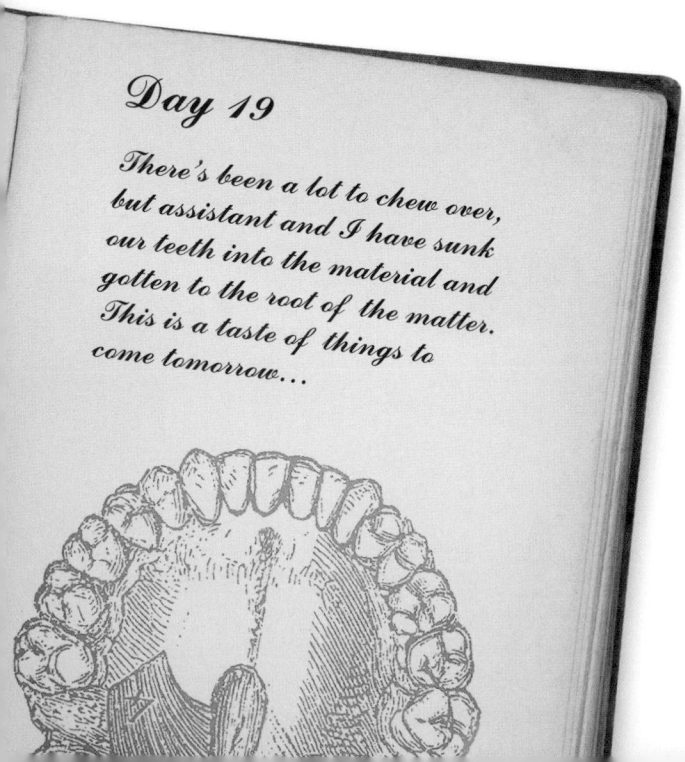

Day 19

There's been a lot to chew over, but assistant and I have sunk our teeth into the material and gotten to the root of the matter. This is a taste of things to come tomorrow...

tooth bacteria

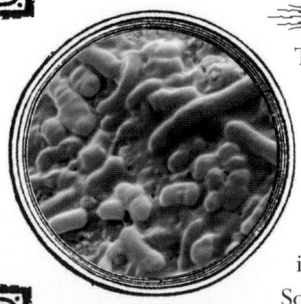

These bacteria live on the surface of a tooth. If you don't brush your teeth daily, bacteria and old food form a sticky mixture called plaque. The bacteria release acids as they feed, which can eat into enamel and cause tooth decay. So, brush those teeth!

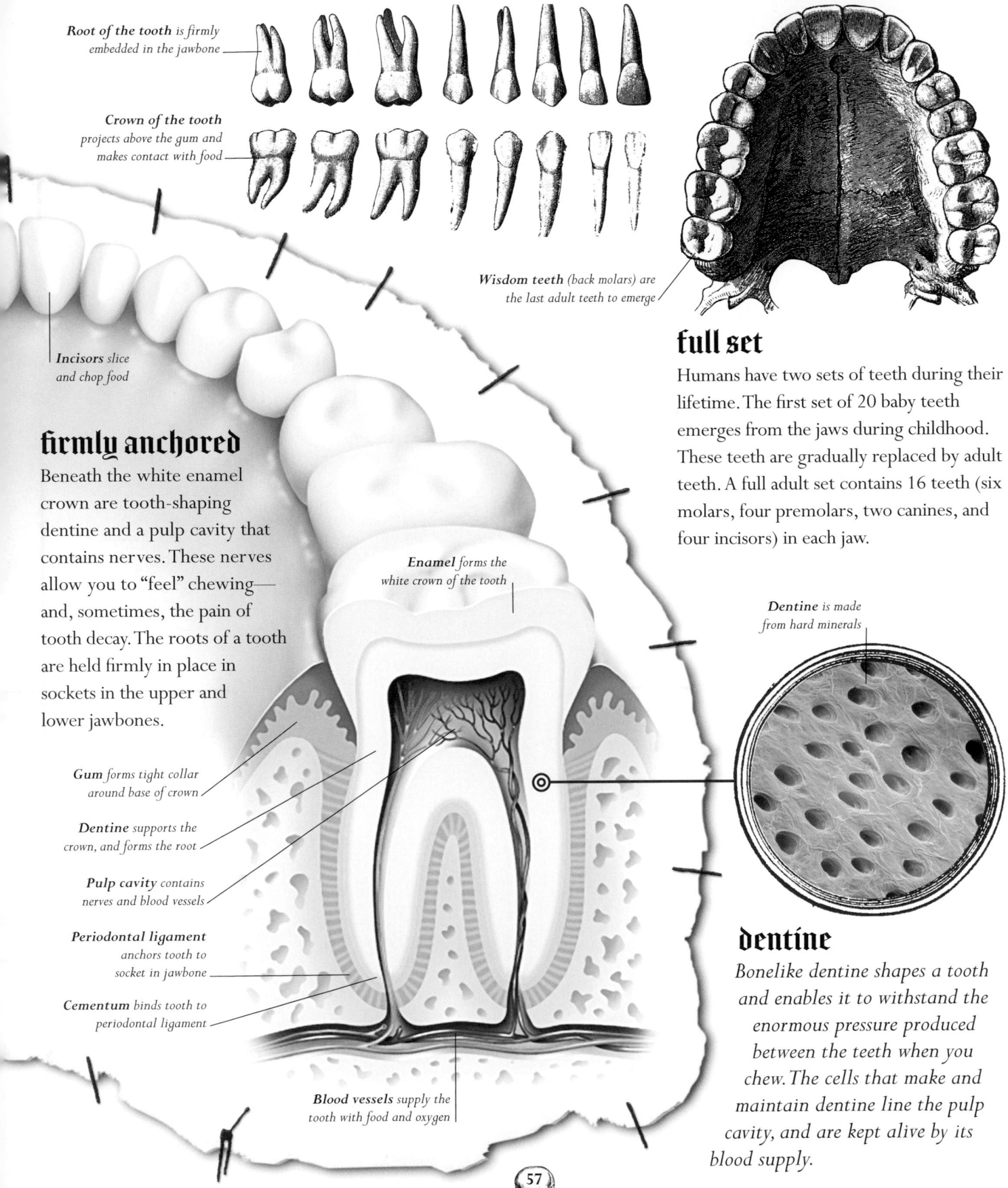

full set

Humans have two sets of teeth during their lifetime. The first set of 20 baby teeth emerges from the jaws during childhood. These teeth are gradually replaced by adult teeth. A full adult set contains 16 teeth (six molars, four premolars, two canines, and four incisors) in each jaw.

firmly anchored

Beneath the white enamel crown are tooth-shaping dentine and a pulp cavity that contains nerves. These nerves allow you to "feel" chewing—and, sometimes, the pain of tooth decay. The roots of a tooth are held firmly in place in sockets in the upper and lower jawbones.

dentine

Bonelike dentine shapes a tooth and enables it to withstand the enormous pressure produced between the teeth when you chew. The cells that make and maintain dentine line the pulp cavity, and are kept alive by its blood supply.

Mouth, throat, and esophagus

Before we can put food inside the mouth, the body needs to be ready to make use of the food's nutrients. This process is called digestion. It occurs when food passes along a long tube called the alimentary canal, which begins with the mouth, throat, and esophagus.

tongue

The tongue is covered with three types of tiny bumps called papillae. Big circumvallate papillae and more numerous, mushroom-shaped fungiform papillae house taste buds. Spiky filiform papillae grip food as it is chewed, and also detect the food's texture and temperature.

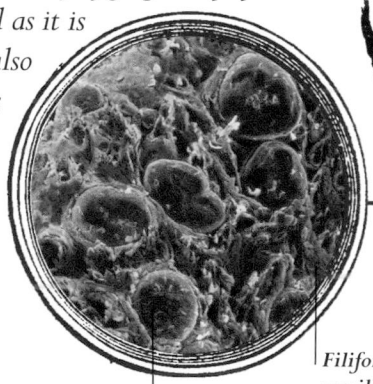

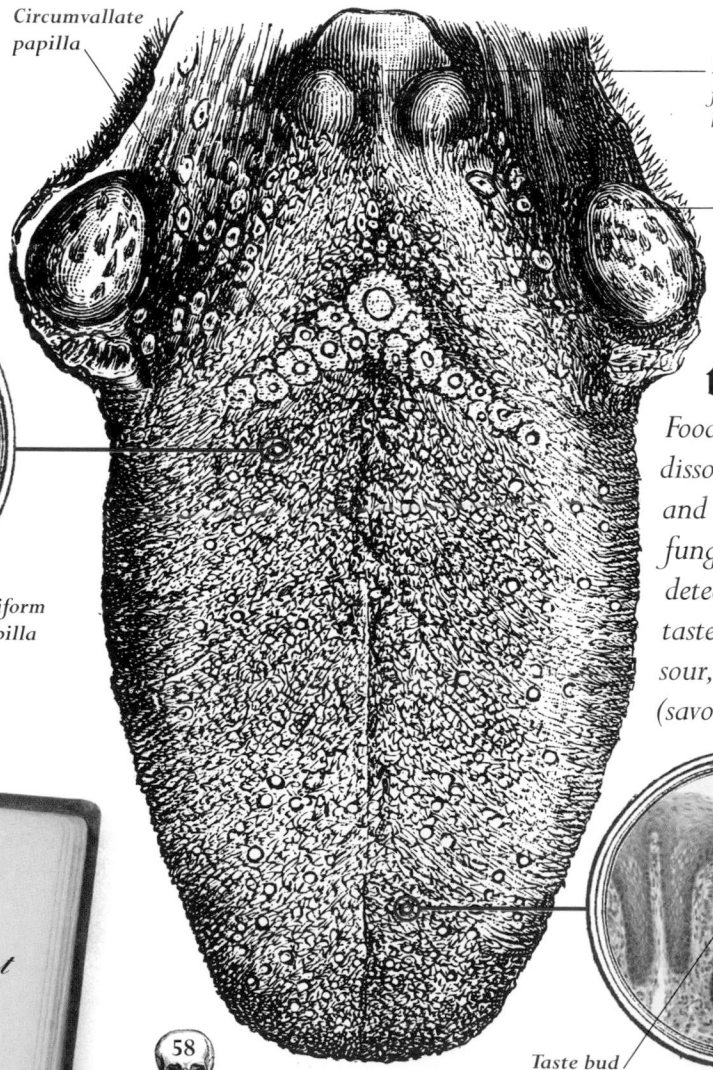

taste

Food molecules dissolve in saliva, and taste buds in the fungiform papillae detect their basic tastes—sweet, sour, salty, umami (savory), or bitter.

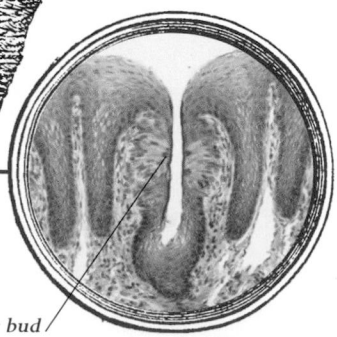

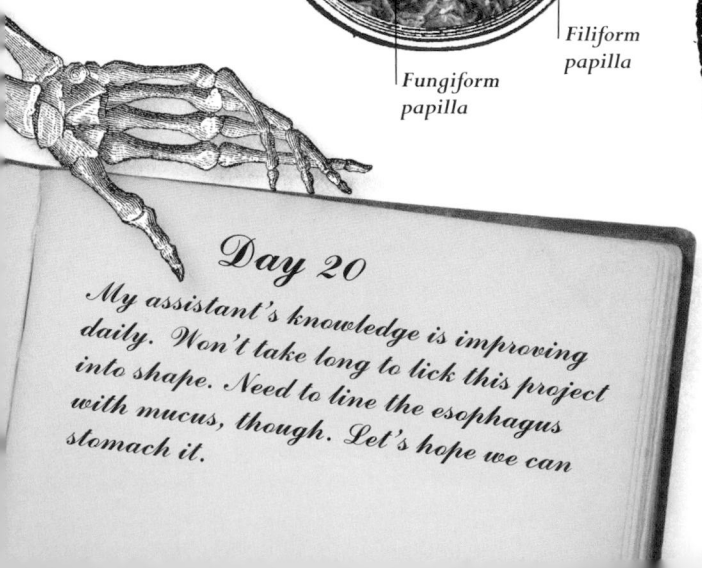

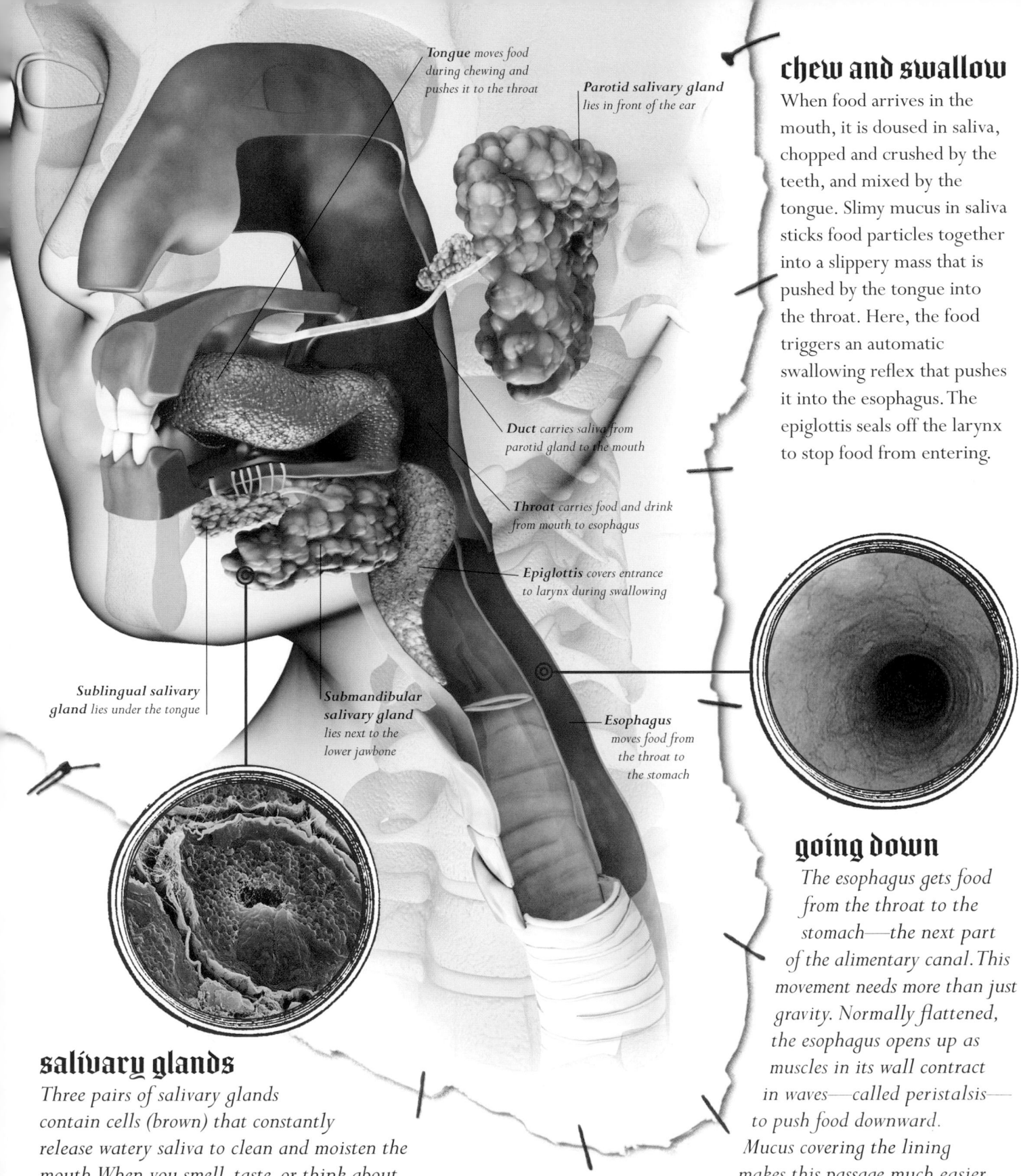

chew and swallow

When food arrives in the mouth, it is doused in saliva, chopped and crushed by the teeth, and mixed by the tongue. Slimy mucus in saliva sticks food particles together into a slippery mass that is pushed by the tongue into the throat. Here, the food triggers an automatic swallowing reflex that pushes it into the esophagus. The epiglottis seals off the larynx to stop food from entering.

salivary glands

Three pairs of salivary glands contain cells (brown) that constantly release watery saliva to clean and moisten the mouth. When you smell, taste, or think about food, the salivary glands go into overdrive.

going down

The esophagus gets food from the throat to the stomach—the next part of the alimentary canal. This movement needs more than just gravity. Normally flattened, the esophagus opens up as muscles in its wall contract in waves—called peristalsis—to push food downward. Mucus covering the lining makes this passage much easier.

Stomach

Now it's time to install the stomach at the end of the esophagus. Here, swallowed food will be stored, liquidized, and released in small amounts to continue its journey down the alimentary canal.

gatekeeper

The pyloric sphincter is the stomach's own gatekeeper. This ring of muscle controls the flow of creamy, part-digested food from the stomach into the duodenum, the next part of the alimentary canal. It is usually contracted and closed, but relaxes and partially opens from time to time.

folded lining

The volume of the stomach can increase from just 0.1 pints (50 ml) when empty, to a massive 8½ pints (4 liters), after a big meal. It can expand because of big folds in its lining.

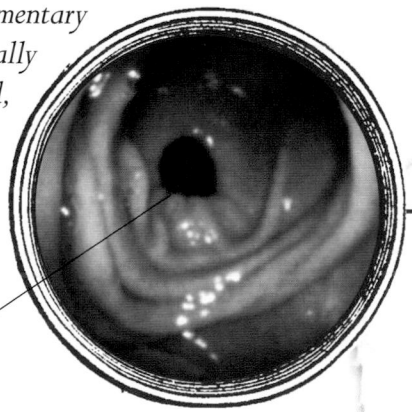

Pyloric sphincter *slightly open, showing the duodenum beyond*

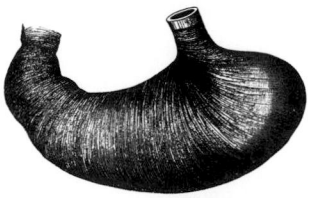

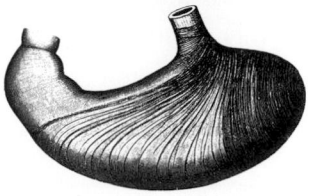

Duodenum *is the first section of the small intestine*

muscular bag

The J-shaped stomach is the widest part of the alimentary canal. It is very elastic, and can expand enormously after a meal. It has three layers of smooth muscles in its wall—other parts of the alimentary canal only have two—to pummel food into a creamy paste called chyme.

Protective membrane *covers the stomach and other parts of the alimentary canal*

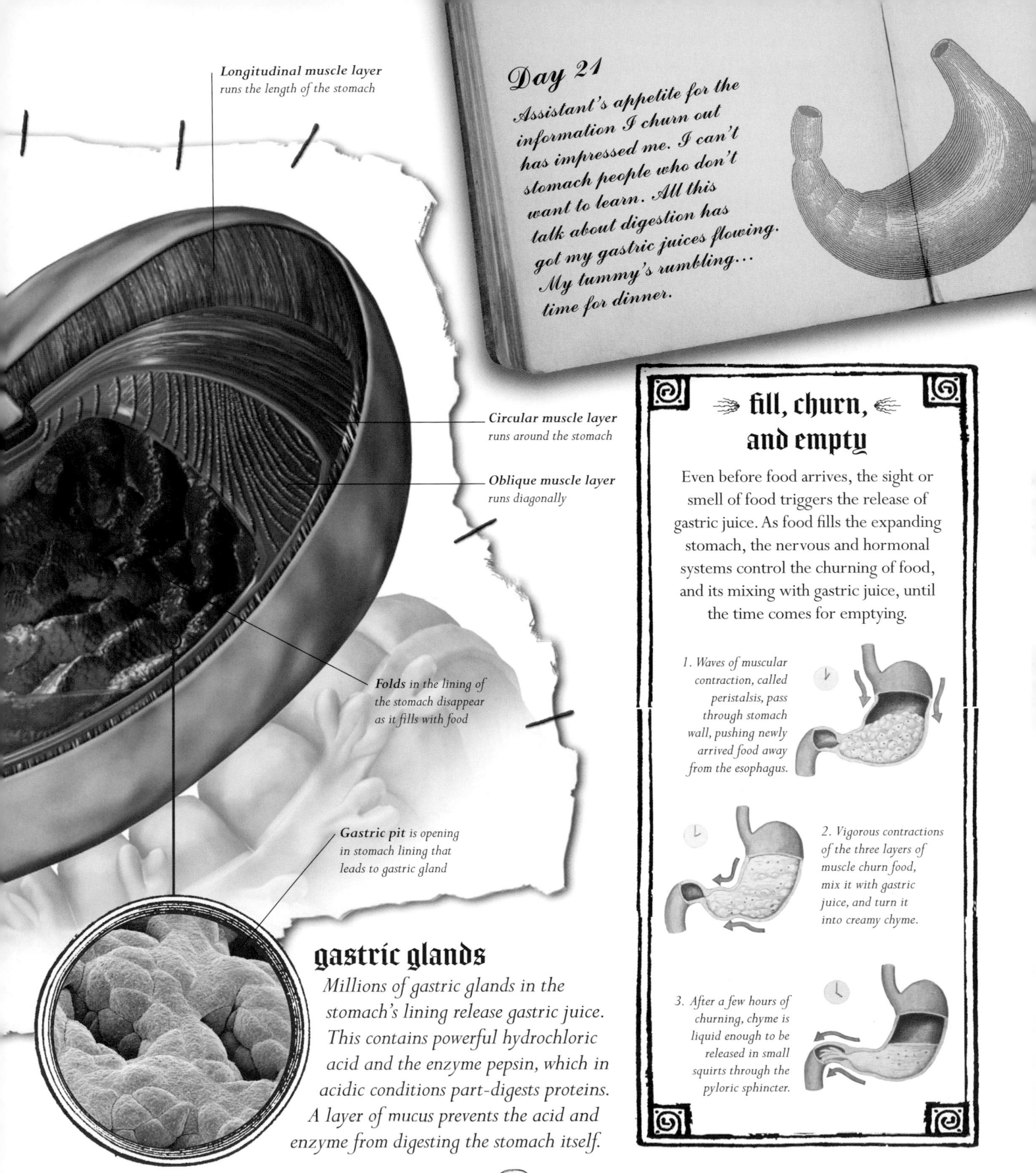
Longitudinal muscle layer
runs the length of the stomach
Day 21
Assistant's appetite for the information I churn out has impressed me. I can't stomach people who don't want to learn. All this talk about digestion has got my gastric juices flowing. My tummy's rumbling... time for dinner.
Circular muscle layer
runs around the stomach
Oblique muscle layer
runs diagonally
Folds in the lining of the stomach disappear as it fills with food
Gastric pit is opening in stomach lining that leads to gastric gland
gastric glands
Millions of gastric glands in the stomach's lining release gastric juice. This contains powerful hydrochloric acid and the enzyme pepsin, which in acidic conditions part-digests proteins. A layer of mucus prevents the acid and enzyme from digesting the stomach itself.
fill, churn, and empty
Even before food arrives, the sight or smell of food triggers the release of gastric juice. As food fills the expanding stomach, the nervous and hormonal systems control the churning of food, and its mixing with gastric juice, until the time comes for emptying.
1. Waves of muscular contraction, called peristalsis, pass through stomach wall, pushing newly arrived food away from the esophagus.
2. Vigorous contractions of the three layers of muscle churn food, mix it with gastric juice, and turn it into creamy chyme.
3. After a few hours of churning, chyme is liquid enough to be released in small squirts through the pyloric sphincter.

Intestines

We finish off the alimentary canal by plumbing in the small and large intestines into a limited space inside the abdomen. It's here that the breakdown of major food groups—carbohydrates, fats, and proteins—into simple, usable nutrients is completed. Leftover waste is also removed.

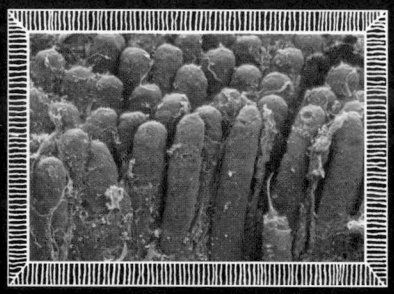

A carpet of fingerlike villi, each about 0.03 in (1 mm) long, lines the small intestine.

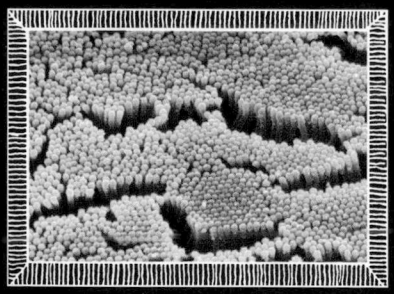

A mass of microvilli greatly increases the surface area of a villus cell for digestion and absorption.

villi

Each villus contains a blood capillary network that carries away glucose and amino acids, as well as lymph vessels that carry away fats. The cells that cover villi have their own microscopic projections, called microvilli.

small and large

The small intestine is the longest and most important part of the alimentary canal. Inside, digestion is completed and simple nutrients are absorbed. The shorter, but wider, large intestine—particularly the colon—forms and disposes of feces.

***Duodenum** is the first part of the small intestine*

***Circular folds** inside the small intestine covered by tiny villi*

huge surface

The small intestine has a massive surface area for digesting and absorbing. Circular folds in its lining provide a much bigger internal surface than a flat lining would do. The folds are covered by millions of villi, which carry some digestive enzymes. Others are provided by the pancreas. These enzymes complete the digestion of food into glucose, amino acids, and fatty acids, so that these nutrients can be absorbed into the blood.

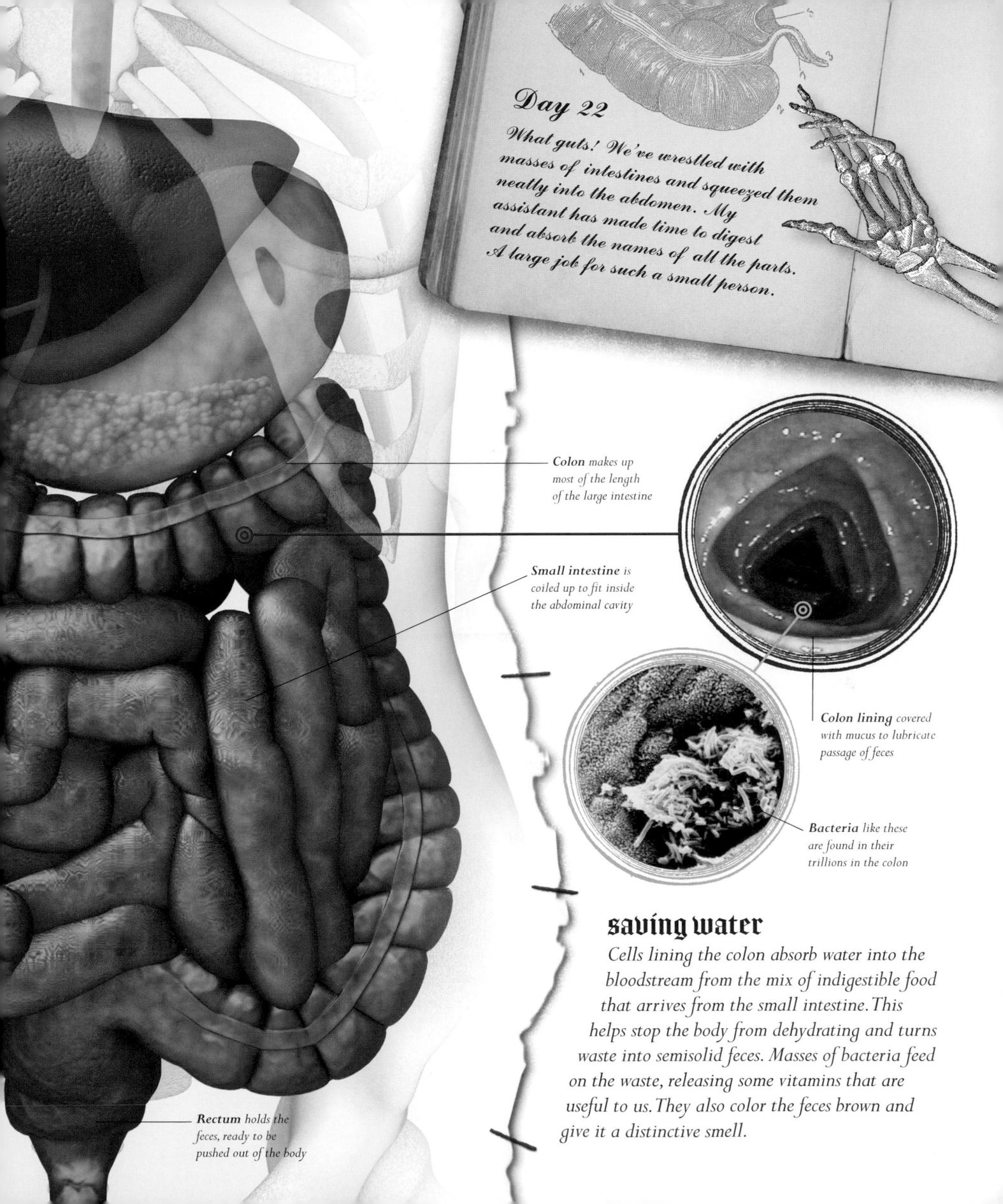

saving water

Cells lining the colon absorb water into the bloodstream from the mix of indigestible food that arrives from the small intestine. This helps stop the body from dehydrating and turns waste into semisolid feces. Masses of bacteria feed on the waste, releasing some vitamins that are useful to us. They also color the feces brown and give it a distinctive smell.

Liver and pancreas

Now it's time to insert the liver and pancreas. The liver takes up most of the space in the top of the abdomen, while the tadpole-shaped pancreas nestles beneath the stomach. Without the bile and pancreatic juice these two organs release, digestion wouldn't work properly.

***Liver** is the body's largest internal organ*

***Gall bladder** stores bile*

liver cells

These masters of multitasking perform more than 500 vital functions. In addition to making bile, liver cells process, store, and dispatch newly absorbed nutrients so that the right levels of these substances remain in the blood. They also rid the blood of poisonous chemicals.

***Sheets of liver cells** seen greatly magnified, surrounding large capillaries*

***Liver cells** are arranged around branches of blood vessels*

***Gall bladder** is tucked behind the liver*

***Duodenum** receives bile and pancreatic juice*

bile and juice

Both bile and pancreatic juice are released along ducts that merge before emptying into the duodenum. Made by the liver, bile is a mixture of bile salts, which play a part in fat digestion, and waste products. Pancreatic juice is produced by the pancreas and contains enzymes that break down fats, proteins, and carbohydrates in food into simpler substances.

Day 23

Today, assistant had the gall to ask me whether the liver is important. That certainly stirred up my juices! Of course it is, and so is the pancreas. Without them the digestive system just wouldn't be complete.

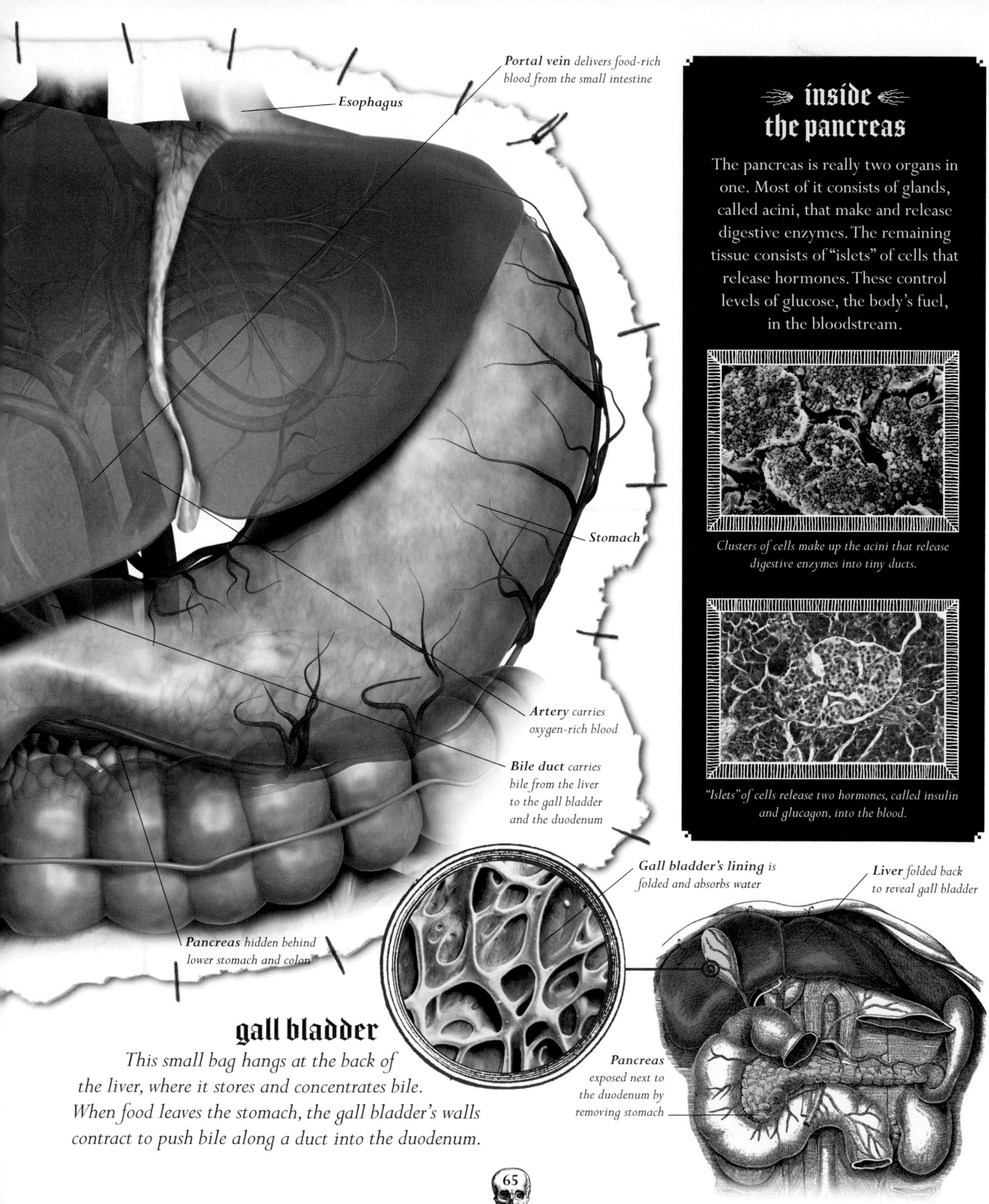

inside the pancreas

The pancreas is really two organs in one. Most of it consists of glands, called acini, that make and release digestive enzymes. The remaining tissue consists of "islets" of cells that release hormones. These control levels of glucose, the body's fuel, in the bloodstream.

Clusters of cells make up the acini that release digestive enzymes into tiny ducts.

"Islets" of cells release two hormones, called insulin and glucagon, into the blood.

gall bladder

This small bag hangs at the back of the liver, where it stores and concentrates bile. When food leaves the stomach, the gall bladder's walls contract to push bile along a duct into the duodenum.

Digestive system

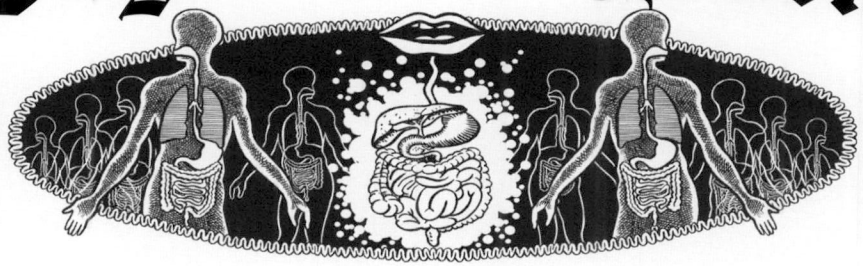

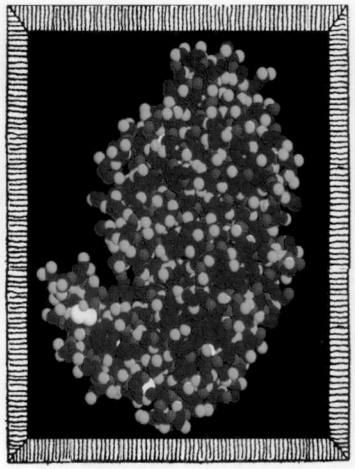

At last, we've assembled all the sections of the alimentary canal, and added the liver and pancreas to make the digestive system. Its job is to break down the big molecules in food into small molecules that the body can use.

Food *takes 10 seconds to travel down the esophagus from throat to stomach*

Stomach *churns food for about three hours—more if it contains lots of fat*

Small intestine *takes about six hours to complete digestion*

Watery waste *is dried out to form feces after 12 to 36 hours in the large intestine*

slow process

The alimentary canal is about 29 ft (9 m) from mouth to anus. It takes hours for food to be pushed along the canal by muscular movement, but that allows plenty of time for food to be completely digested and absorbed.

Food *is chewed, crushed, and mixed with saliva in the mouth*

Salivary glands *release saliva, which contains a starch-digesting enzyme*

chemical digesters

Digestion would be impossible without enzymes. These chemical digesters increase (by thousands or millions of times) the rate at which food is broken down into nutrients. This enzyme (above), called pepsin, is released into the stomach to break down proteins.

food processor

Whether it's starchy carbohydrates in pasta, proteins in fish, or fats in peanuts, your digestive system can process it. Food is crushed and churned by the teeth and stomach walls. Enzyme action in the mouth, stomach, and small intestine converts crushed food into simple nutrients—glucose, amino acids, and fatty acids—perfect for energy, growth, and repair.

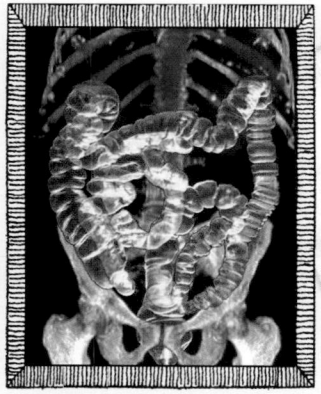

gut scan

This remarkable scan shows the guts (intestines) of a living person. What it desn't show you is the 4 lb (2 kg) of friendly bacteria that live in the colon, feed on waste, and make farts.

Esophagus *pushes food to the stomach using waves of smooth muscle contraction, called peristalsis*

Liver *processes absorbed food and releases bile to aid fat digestion*

Stomach muscles *contract to churn food, and liquidize it by mixing it with gastric juice*

Small intestine *is where digestion is completed and absorption of simple nutrients takes place*

Anus *is the exit point for feces*

Colon, *the longest part of the large intestine, produces and stores feces*

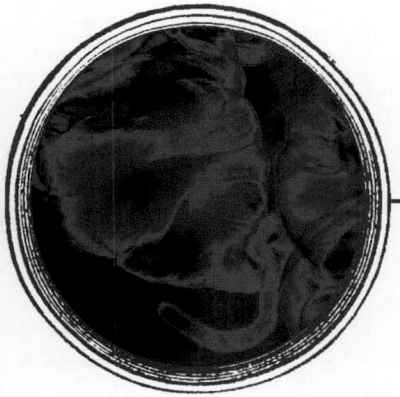

appendix

The appendix is a blind-ending tube that extends from the first part of the large intestine. It was believed for many years to have no role at all, but now some scientists think it plays a part in defense against disease.

Day 24

It's been a lot to digest, but assistant now appreciates what happens between food going in one end and waste coming out of the other. What is that stomach-churning smell, by the way? Assistant seems to know a lot about bad gases, too!

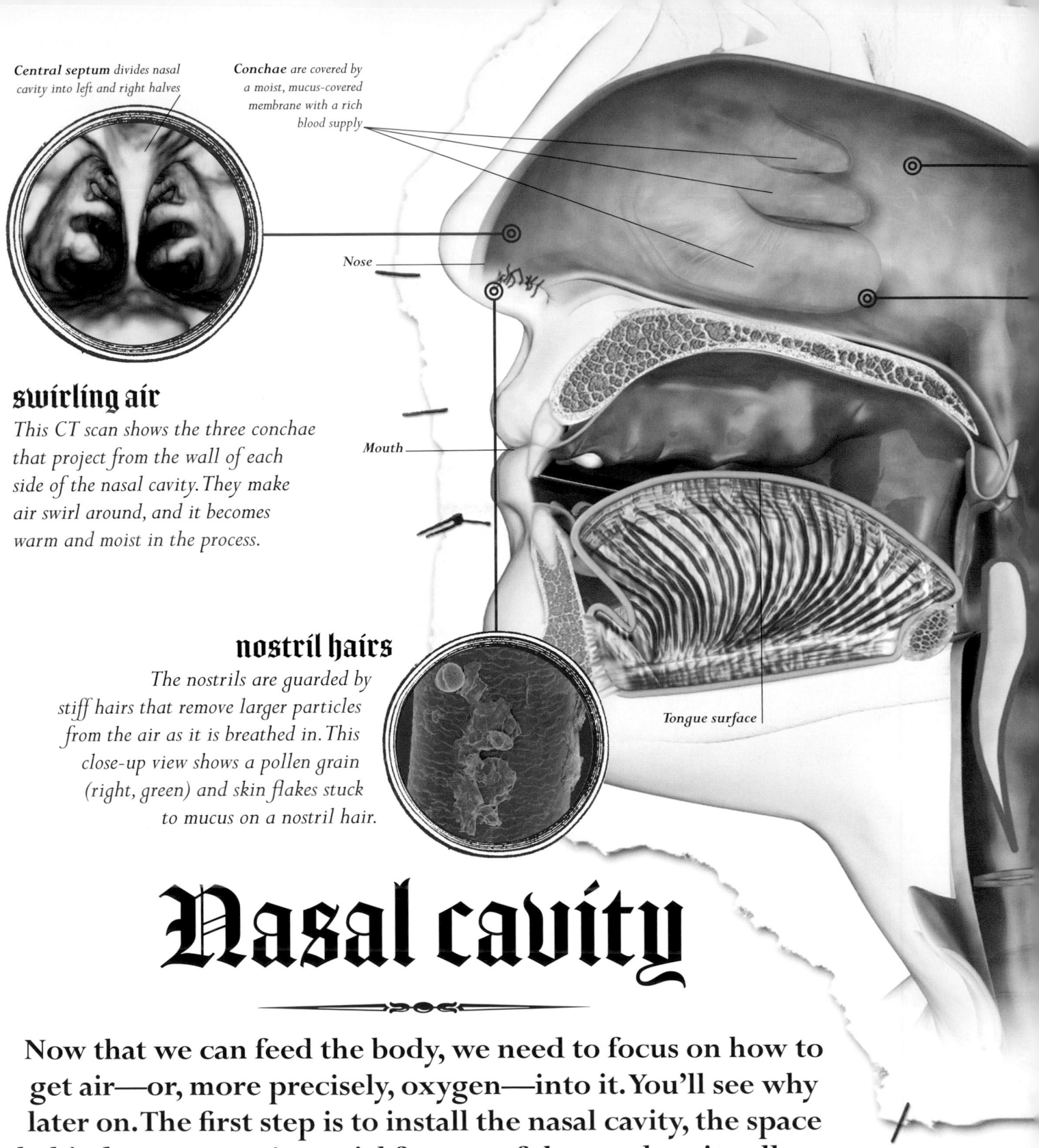

swirling air

This CT scan shows the three conchae that project from the wall of each side of the nasal cavity. They make air swirl around, and it becomes warm and moist in the process.

nostril hairs

The nostrils are guarded by stiff hairs that remove larger particles from the air as it is breathed in. This close-up view shows a pollen grain (right, green) and skin flakes stuck to mucus on a nostril hair.

Nasal cavity

Now that we can feed the body, we need to focus on how to get air—or, more precisely, oxygen—into it. You'll see why later on. The first step is to install the nasal cavity, the space behind your nose. A special feature of the nasal cavity allows you to smell everything from roses to rotten eggs.

smell detectors

At the top of each side of the nasal cavity is a patch of lining called the olfactory (smell) epithelium. Within it are odor receptor cells. These respond when smell molecules in the air dissolve in the watery mucus that covers them.

stick and waft

Some cells lining the nasal cavity produce sticky mucus. Others have hairlike cilia on their outer surfaces. Particles and pathogens in the swirling air stick to the mucus. Cilia sway backward and forward to waft dirt-laden mucus to the throat, where it is swallowed and digested.

***Cilia** in the nasal cavity lining move mucus*

inside the nose

The nasal cavity is a wind tunnel that carries air from the two nostrils to the throat. En route, the air is warmed, moistened, and filtered to remove particles and pathogens that might cause damage deeper inside the body.

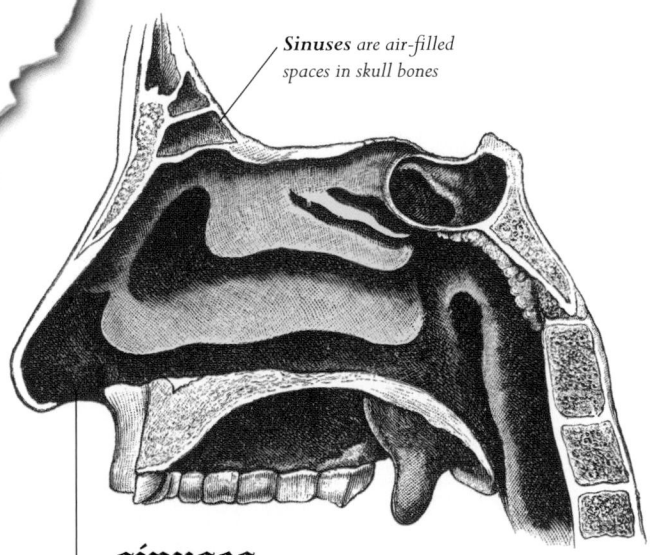

sinuses

Connected to the nasal cavity and lined with the same moist membrane, sinuses serve to make the skull lighter. They also help to moisten and warm air, and make our voices sound the way they do.

Section through olfactory bulb and olfactory epithelium

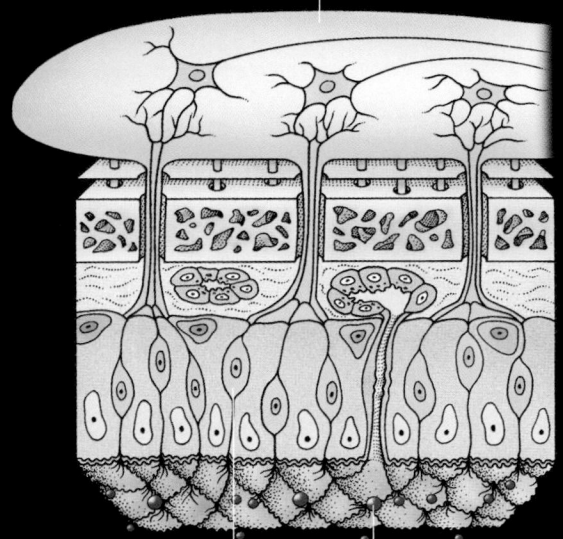

nose to brain

Smell receptors are found here in the nasal cavity, in a piece of tissue called the olfactory epithelium. Each receptor cell responds to odor molecules in the air by sending signals to the brain. By analyzing input from smell receptors, the brain can distinguish between 10,000 different smells.

Larynx, trachea, and bronchi

It's time to install and connect the airways. Where did I put that pile of tubes? The trachea and bronchi are straightforward. It's when the bronchi start branching out into the lungs that things get more complicated.

voice box

The funnellike larynx links the throat and trachea and is made of several pieces of cartilage. In addition to being an air passage, the larynx also contains the sound-producing vocal cords, hence its alternative name—the voice box.

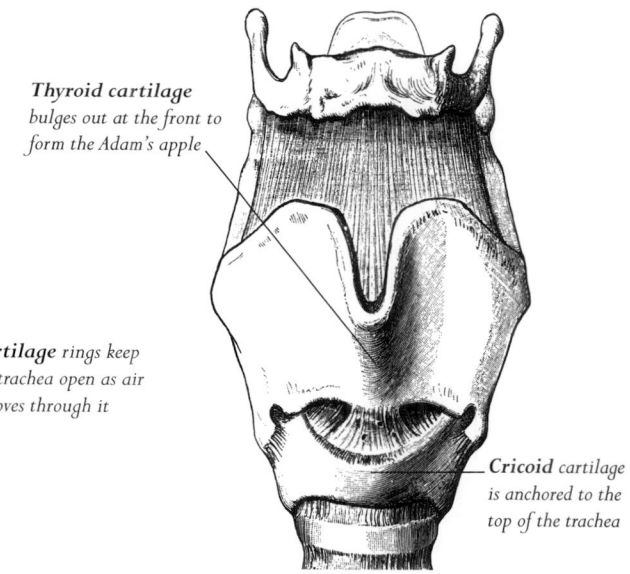

windpipe

Look down the trachea, or windpipe, of a living person and you'll see its pink lining covered with slimy mucus. Those ridges are formed by C-shaped cartilage rings, which stop the trachea from collapsing inward when air whooshes through it.

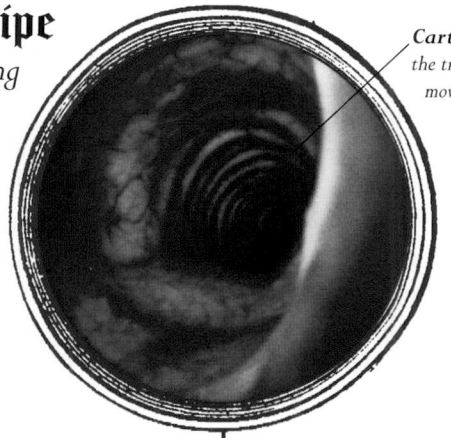

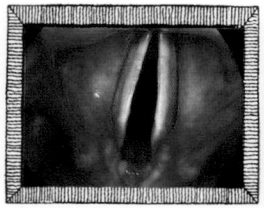

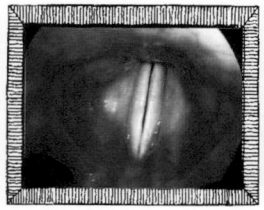

making sounds

Two membranes, the vocal cords, cross the larynx. Normally, they're open. When they close, they vibrate as air passes through them, producing sounds that are turned into speech.

airways

These tubes carry air into and out of the chest. At the base of the throat, the larynx leads to the trachea, which branches into two bronchi. These divide many times to form tiny bronchioles. It's like an upside-down "tree," with the trachea as the trunk, bronchi as branches, and bronchioles as twigs.

Trachea is a flexible tube that links larynx to bronchi

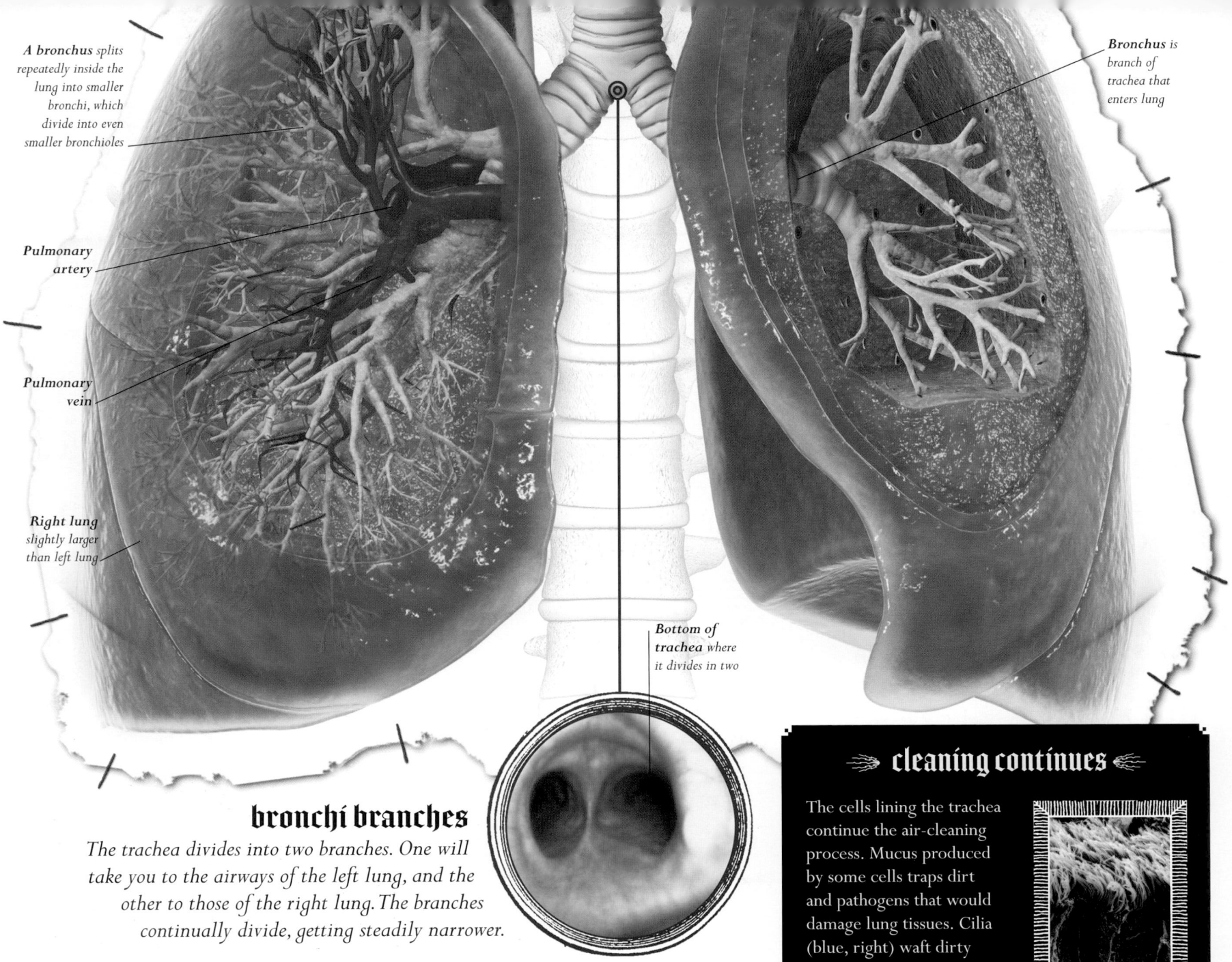

bronchi branches

The trachea divides into two branches. One will take you to the airways of the left lung, and the other to those of the right lung. The branches continually divide, getting steadily narrower.

cleaning continues

The cells lining the trachea continue the air-cleaning process. Mucus produced by some cells traps dirt and pathogens that would damage lung tissues. Cilia (blue, right) waft dirty mucus up to the throat, where it is swallowed.

Lungs

At the center of the respiratory system are the lungs. Packed with air-filled passages and bags, these two spongy organs play a vital part in helping to exchange oxygen for unwanted carbon dioxide. Take a deep breath and let's get started.

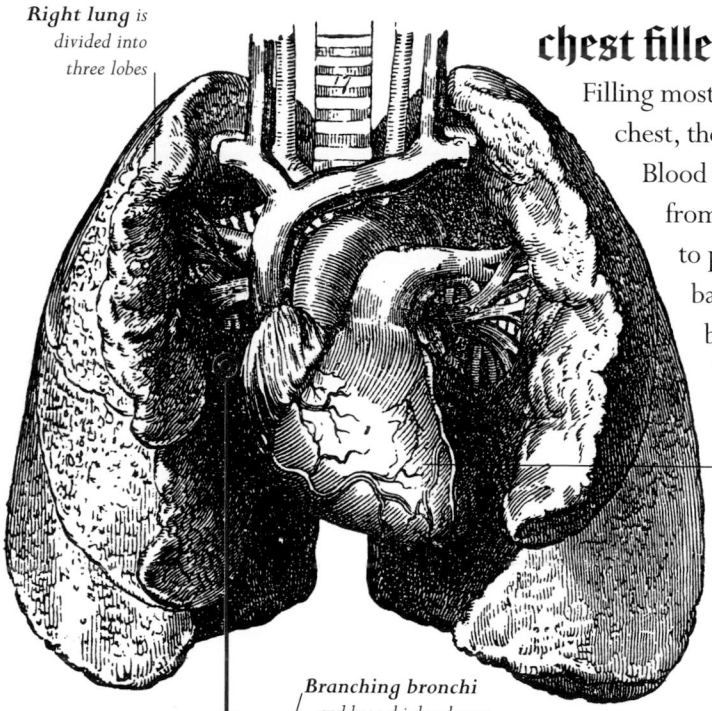

chest fillers

Filling most of the space inside the chest, the lungs surround the heart. Blood travels a short distance from the heart to the lungs to pick up oxygen, then back to the heart to be pumped to body cells.

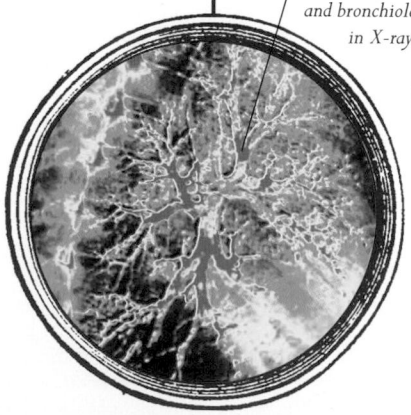

bronchi to bronchioles

The single bronchus entering each lung divides into smaller bronchi that branch into even smaller bronchi. These small bronchi split into tiny tubes called bronchioles. The smallest branches of bronchioles end in the alveoli.

clean up

Although we've tried to ensure that air is cleaned as it passes through the nasal cavity, trachea, and bronchi, some tiny particles still get through. Help is at hand, however. Macrophages (right, pink) inside alveoli surround and eat dust particles (green) to keep the airways clear.

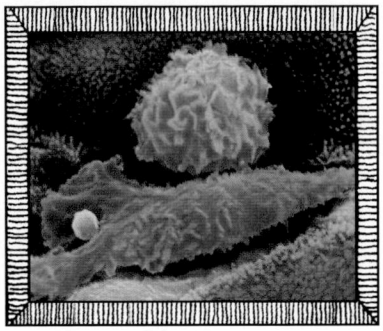

rib protection

Assisted by the backbone and sternum (breastbone), 12 pairs of ribs form a protective cage. They surround the lungs as well as the heart and major blood vessels that we've already installed. And, as you'll soon find out, the ribs play a key part in breathing.

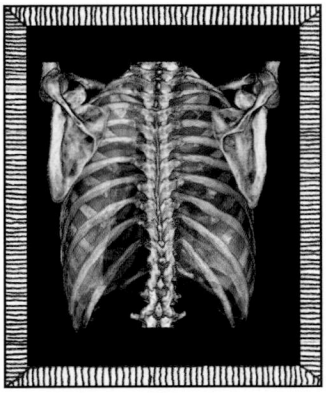

CT scan of chest from the rear showing lungs (blue) surrounded by ribs.

Alveoli are arranged into bunches like grapes

air bags

The finest bronchiole branches lead to air bags called alveoli. Through their moist linings, oxygen from the air passes into the bloodstream, while waste carbon dioxide passes in the opposite direction. Together, the 300 million alveoli in both lungs provide a massive surface area for this exchange of gases.

***Branch of pulmonary artery** delivers oxygen-poor blood*

***Capillary network** surrounds alveoli*

***Branch of pulmonary vein** takes away oxygen-rich blood*

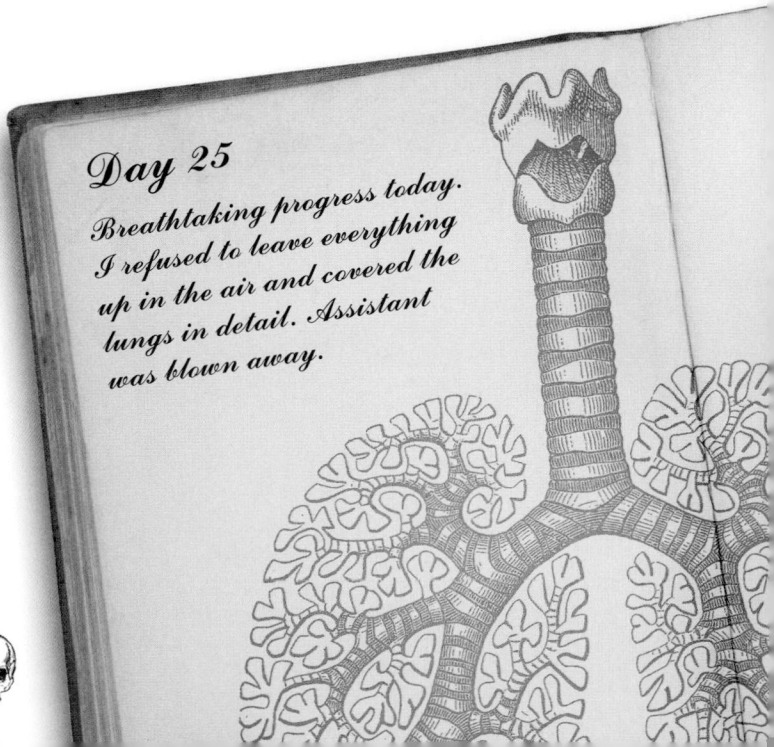

Respiratory system

Air turbulence caused by a sneeze is revealed in this special photograph.

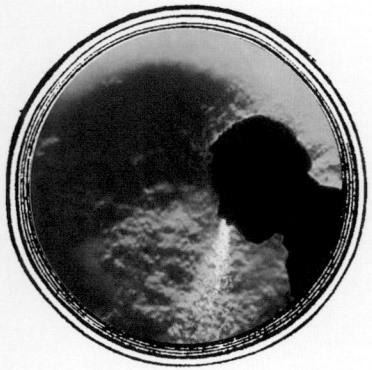

sneezing

Irritations in the nasal cavity are removed by sneezing. Air builds up behind the vocal cords and is suddenly released. This blasts air at high speed through the nasal passages and out through the nostrils.

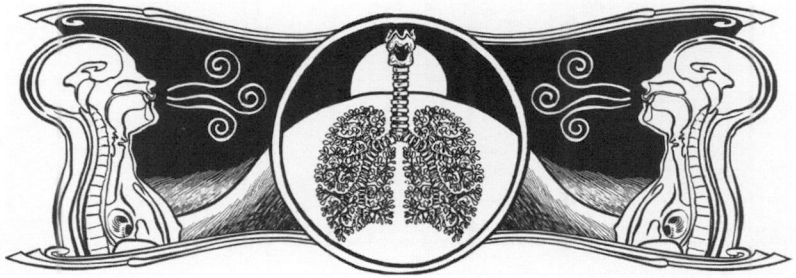

Our complete respiratory system gets oxygen into the body and removes carbon dioxide. Cells need a nonstop supply of oxygen to release the energy that keeps them alive. They also need to get rid of waste carbon dioxide. For all this to happen, air must be moved in and out of the lungs by breathing.

getting oxygen

The lungs are passive "bags" that cannot expand and shrink of their own accord. Getting air into and out of the lungs involves the diaphragm and intercostal muscles. Their activities result in inhalation (breathing in) and exhalation (breathing out).

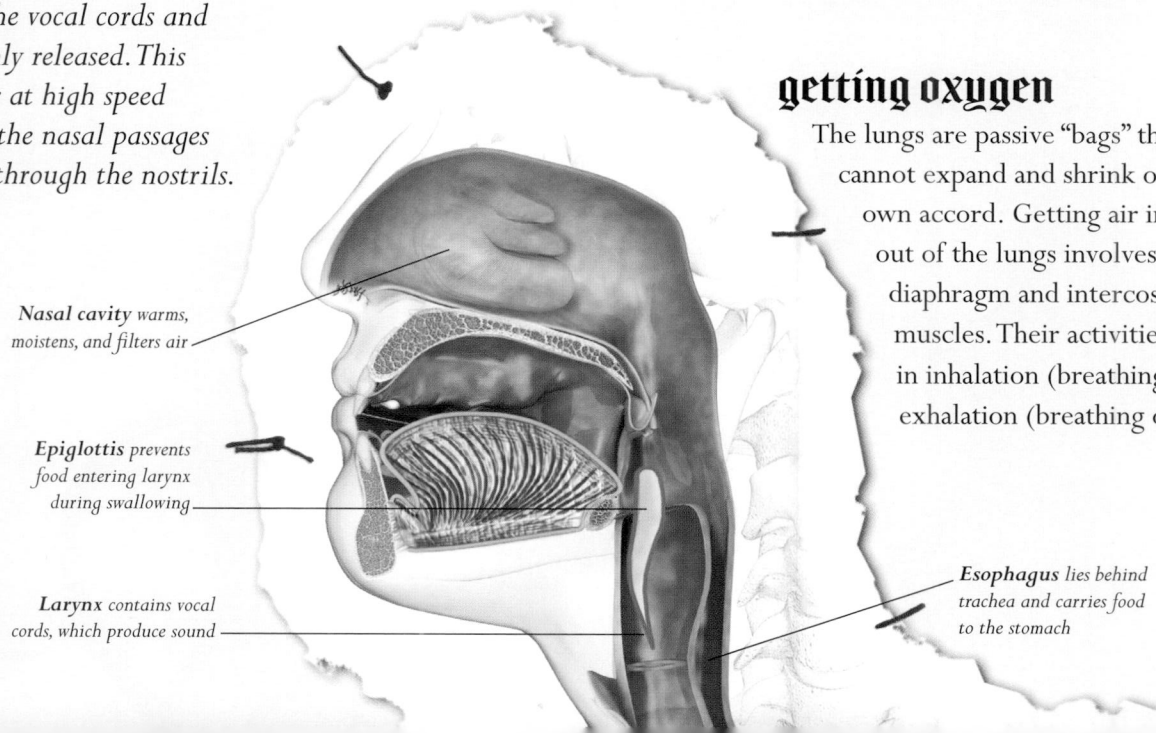

breathing

During inhalation, the diaphragm contracts and flattens, and the intercostal muscles pull the ribs upward and outward. As the chest expands, the lungs follow suit and suck in air. During exhalation, both diaphragm and intercostal muscles relax. The lungs are squeezed, forcing air out.

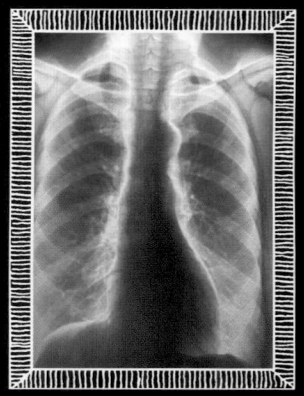

An X-ray of inhalation shows the ribs, lungs (blue), and diaphragm (orange).

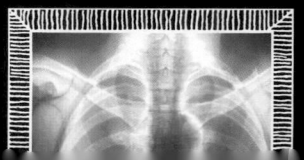

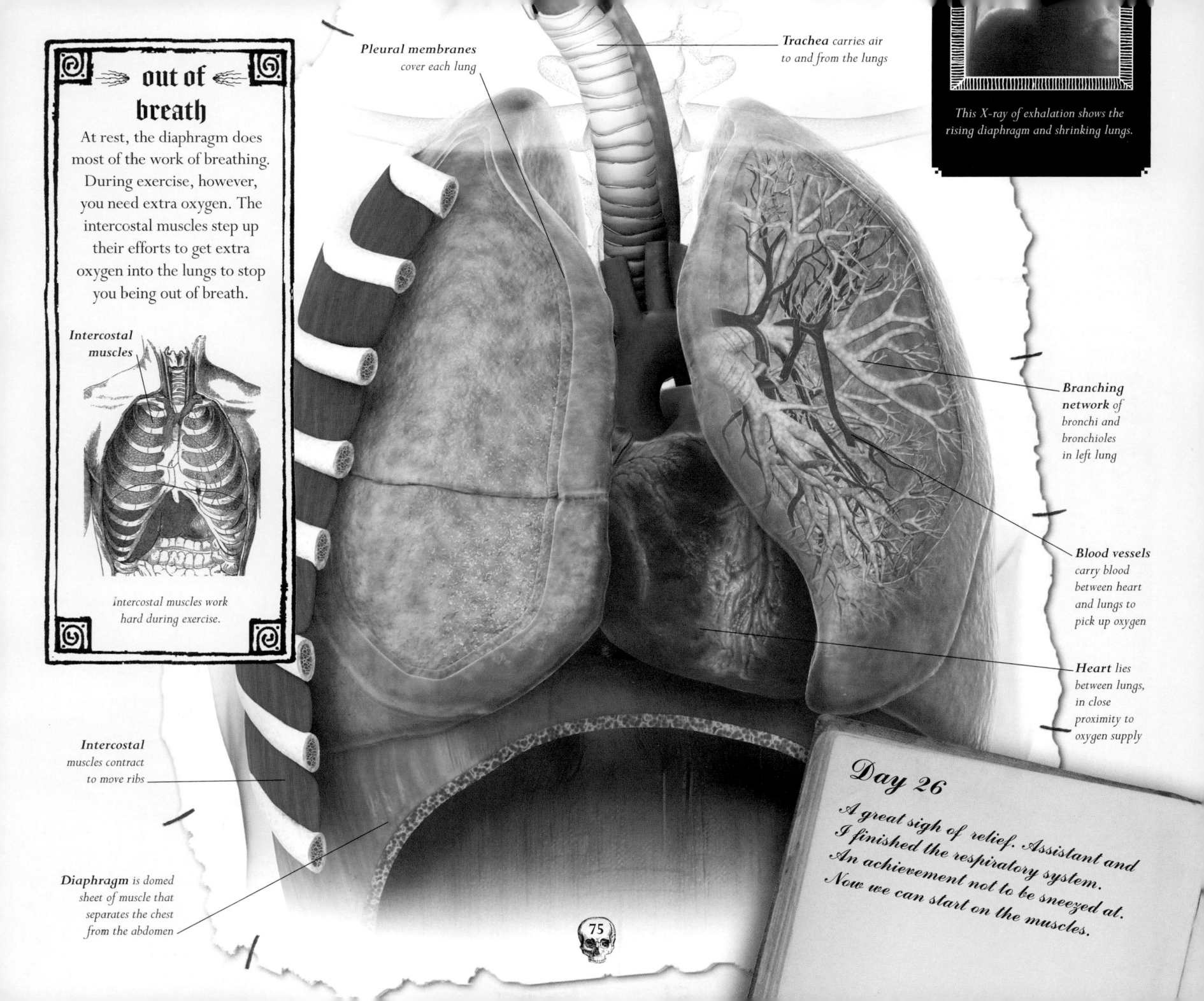
out of breath
At rest, the diaphragm does most of the work of breathing. During exercise, however, you need extra oxygen. The intercostal muscles step up their efforts to get extra oxygen into the lungs to stop you being out of breath.
Intercostal muscles
intercostal muscles work hard during exercise.
Pleural membranes cover each lung
Trachea carries air to and from the lungs
This X-ray of exhalation shows the rising diaphragm and shrinking lungs.
Branching network of bronchi and bronchioles in left lung
Blood vessels carry blood between heart and lungs to pick up oxygen
Heart lies between lungs, in close proximity to oxygen supply
Intercostal muscles contract to move ribs
Diaphragm is domed sheet of muscle that separates the chest from the abdomen
Day 26
A great sigh of relief. Assistant and I finished the respiratory system. An achievement not to be sneezed at. Now we can start on the muscles.
75

Arm and hand muscles

Bone-shifting skeletal muscles enable your limbs to move. These muscles can shorten and pull. Our task today is to equip the chest, back, arms, and hands with muscles and tendons to get those arms swinging and hands gripping.

Pectoralis major *pulls arm forward and rotates it inward*

Deltoid *raises the arm to the side, and swings it backward and forward*

Biceps brachii *bends the arm at the elbow*

Brachioradialis *helps the biceps brachii to bend the arm*

arm movements

To move the arm, you need to use muscles that originate in the upper body, cross the scapula (shoulder), and pull the humerus (upper arm bone). These muscles have plenty of room to maneuver because there's a ball-and-socket joint between the scapula and humerus allowing all-around movement. Muscles that link the shoulder and forearm either bend or straighten the arm.

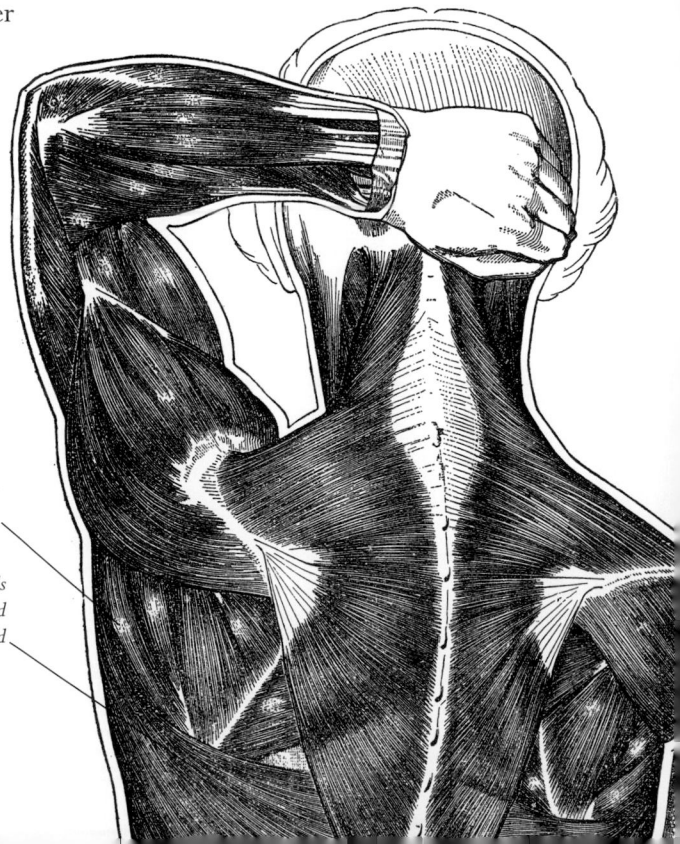

Teres major *aids latissimus dorsi in its arm-moving actions*

Latissimus dorsi *pulls the arm backward and rotates it inward*

wrist and fingers

Many of the hand's movements are produced by forearm muscles. Most muscles in the inner forearm bend the wrist and fingers. Those in the outer forearm generally straighten the wrist and fingers. Note that the forearm muscles are attached to the hand bones by very long tendons.

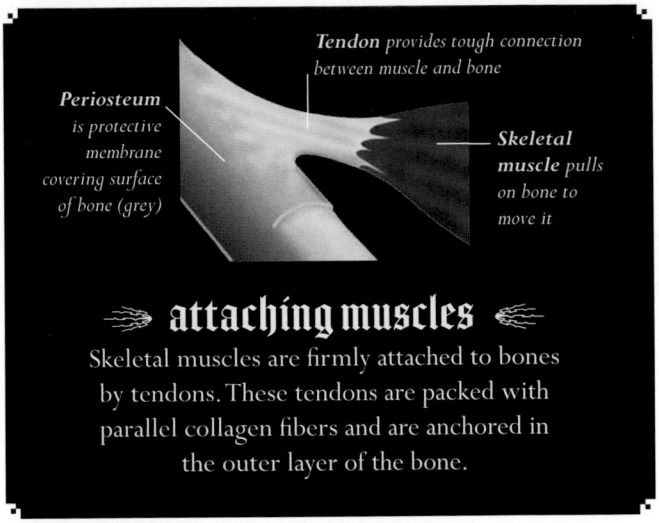

attaching muscles

Skeletal muscles are firmly attached to bones by tendons. These tendons are packed with parallel collagen fibers and are anchored in the outer layer of the bone.

Long tendons *of extensor digitorum muscle*

Flexor carpi ulnaris *bends the hand downward at the wrist*

Extensor digitorum *straightens the fingers*

Extensor carpi ulnaris *straightens the wrist*

Triceps brachii *straightens the arm at the elbow*

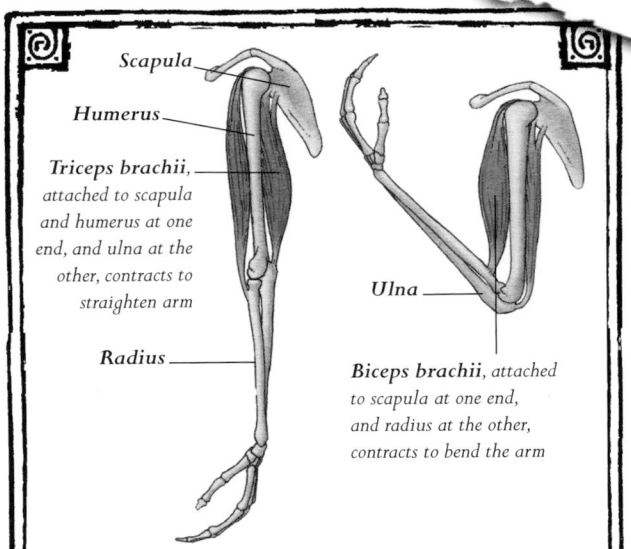

in opposition

It's important for you to realize that muscles contract (get shorter) to pull bones, but they can't actually push bones. So to get movement in two directions, such as bending and straightening the arm, you need two muscles with opposing actions.

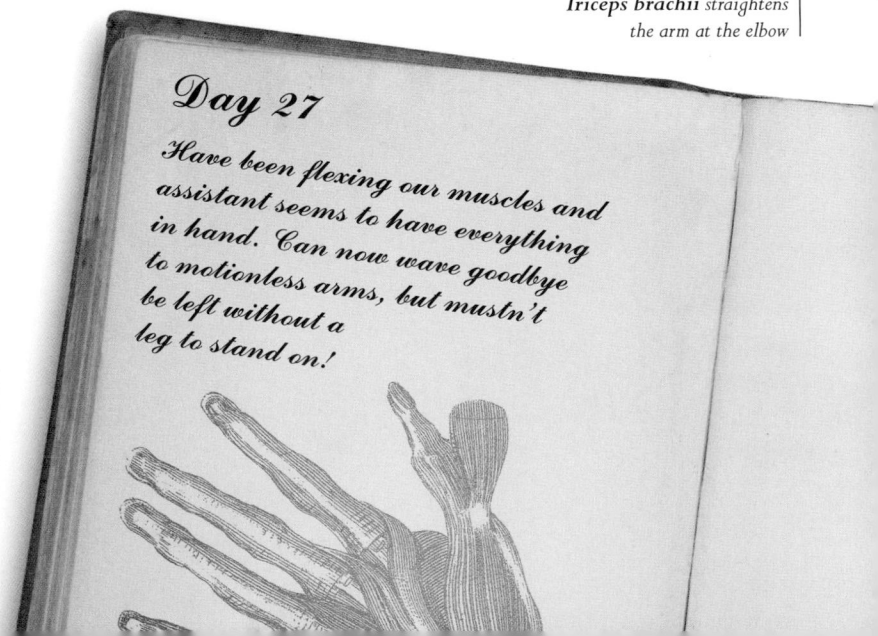

Hip and leg muscles

Ready to move on to the big muscles? Many hip and thigh muscles are bulky because they have to support and move the whole body when you walk or run. Lower leg muscles are powerful, too. Try standing on tiptoe and you can feel your calf muscles at work.

hip and thigh

Thigh muscles are attached to the hip bones at one end, and the femur or lower leg bones at the other. Muscles at the front of the thigh bend the thigh at the hip. The quadriceps femoris also straightens the knee. Muscles at the back of the thigh straighten the thigh at the hip. The hamstrings also bend the knee.

Pectineus *pulls the thigh inward and bends it at the hip*

Iliopsoas *consists of two muscles that bend the thigh at the hip*

Tensor fasciae latae *bends the thigh at the hip and rotates inward*

Adductor longus *pulls and rotates the thigh inward*

Sartorius *bends the thigh at the hip and pulls it outward*

Gluteus maximus *(shown cut) straightens the thigh at the hip*

Gluteus medius *pulls the thigh out to the side and rotates it inward*

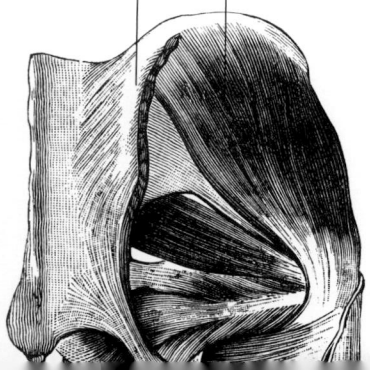

heat generators

When muscles contract, they release heat. This is distributed by the blood and helps the body maintain a steady internal temperature of 98.6°F (37°C), the temperature at which cells work best.

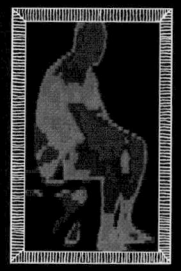

This thermogram, or "heat picture," shows a man at rest.

After exercise, the red, yellow, and white colors show heat is given off.

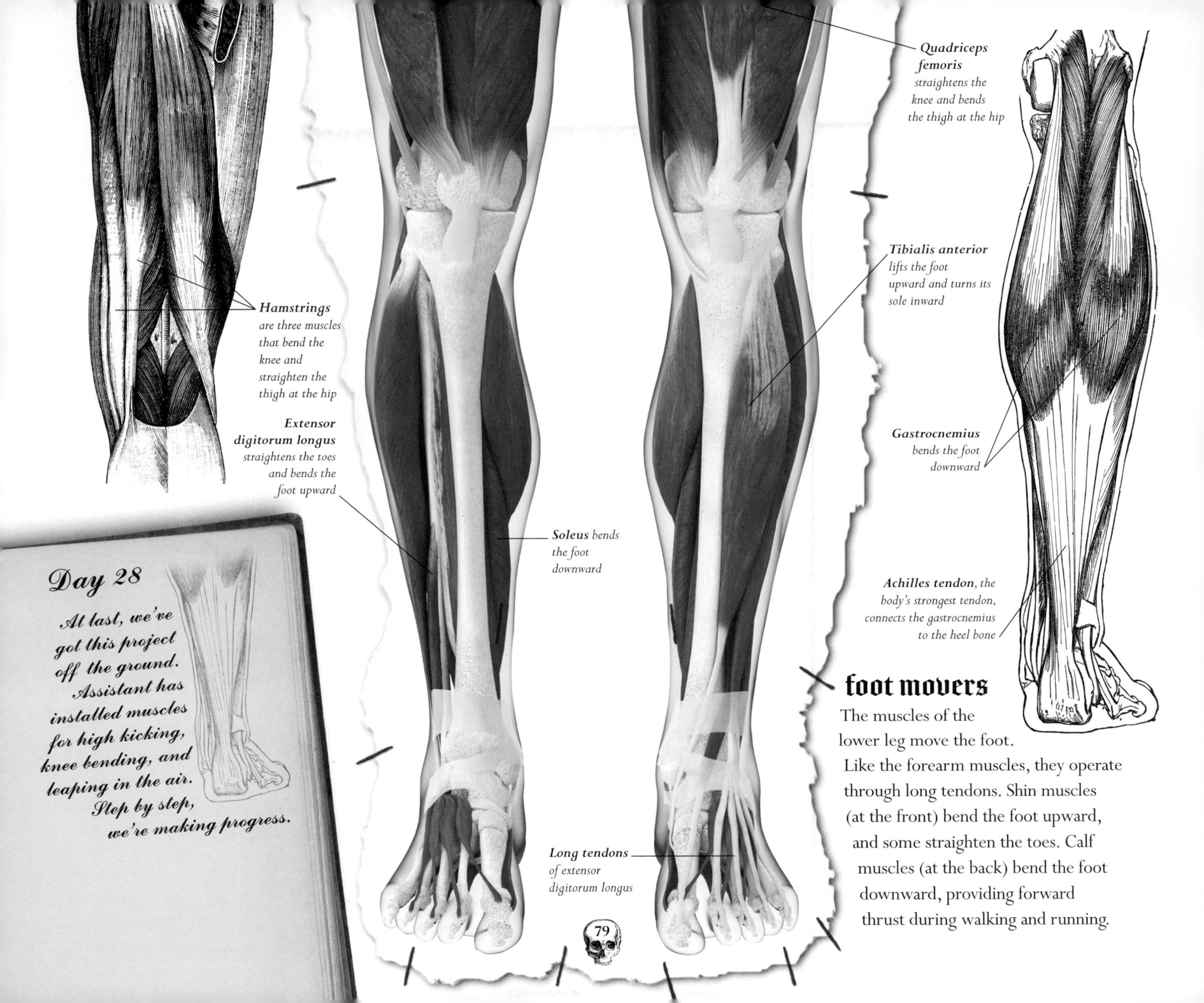

foot movers

The muscles of the lower leg move the foot. Like the forearm muscles, they operate through long tendons. Shin muscles (at the front) bend the foot upward, and some straighten the toes. Calf muscles (at the back) bend the foot downward, providing forward thrust during walking and running.

Head and neck muscles

Our body may be moving, but it hasn't got much of an expression on its face! That will change when we install some facial muscles. Once we get the eyes moving and the jaws chomping, it will be all smiles.

making faces

About 30 facial muscles produce the variety of expressions that communicate our thoughts and emotions. Attached to skull bones, these muscles are unusual because they don't pull bones, but instead tug the skin of the face.

Frontalis *wrinkles forehead and raises eyebrows*

Orbicularis oculi *closes the eye*

Levator labii superioris *raises and curls the upper lip*

Orbicularis oris *purses the lips*

Depressor labii inferioris *pulls lower lip downward*

Depressor anguli oris *pulls corner of the mouth downward*

Mentalis *sticks out the lower lip and wrinkles the chin*

facial expressions

Whether you're smiling or frowning, or looking sad, angry, or surprised, people anywhere in the world can understand what you are feeling from the expression on your face.

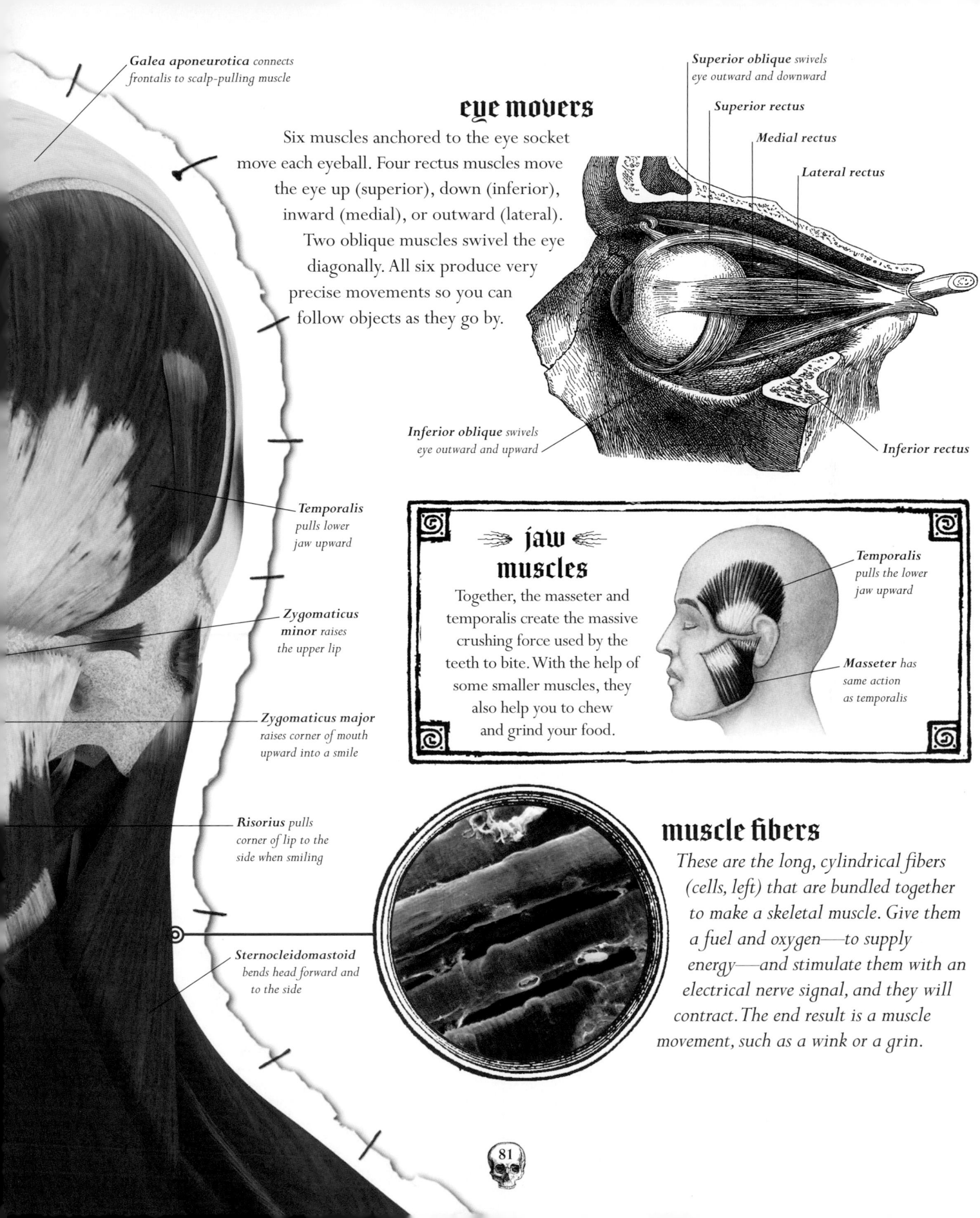

eye movers

Six muscles anchored to the eye socket move each eyeball. Four rectus muscles move the eye up (superior), down (inferior), inward (medial), or outward (lateral). Two oblique muscles swivel the eye diagonally. All six produce very precise movements so you can follow objects as they go by.

jaw muscles

Together, the masseter and temporalis create the massive crushing force used by the teeth to bite. With the help of some smaller muscles, they also help you to chew and grind your food.

muscle fibers

These are the long, cylindrical fibers (cells, left) that are bundled together to make a skeletal muscle. Give them a fuel and oxygen—to supply energy—and stimulate them with an electrical nerve signal, and they will contract. The end result is a muscle movement, such as a wink or a grin.

Muscular system

Now that we have the muscular system in place, you can really see the body shaping up. Remember, though, that these muscles do more than just shape and move us. They also help stabilize joints, hold us upright so we don't collapse in a heap, and release heat to keep our insides warm.

skeletal muscles

If you could count them all, there would be about 650 bone-pulling skeletal muscles in our new creation. They are arranged—as you can see below—in layers ranging from deep to superficial (surface). Muscle names are in Latin and describe a muscle's size, shape, location, or job.

how muscles work

The long, cylindrical fibers, or cells, that make up muscles have a highly organized structure. Each fiber is packed with parallel, rodlike myofibrils. They contain arrays of filaments arranged in a way that gives myofibrils a striped appearance. The filaments interact to make myofibrils, fibers, and the muscle contract.

Orbicularis oculi *closes the eyelids*

Zygomaticus *makes you smile*

Deltoid *raises arm sideways and swings it backward and forward*

Biceps brachii *bends the arm at the elbow*

Frontalis *raises the eyebrows and wrinkles the forehead*

Sternocleidomastoid *bends head forward and turns it to one side*

Pectoralis major *pulls arm forward and toward the body*

Occipitalis *pulls the scalp backward*

Splenius capitis *pulls head backward, turns it to one side, and keeps it upright*

Trapezius *pulls the shoulders and head backward*

Myofibrils *running in parallel (left to right) in this section along a muscle fiber*

Triceps brachii *straightens the arm at the elbow*

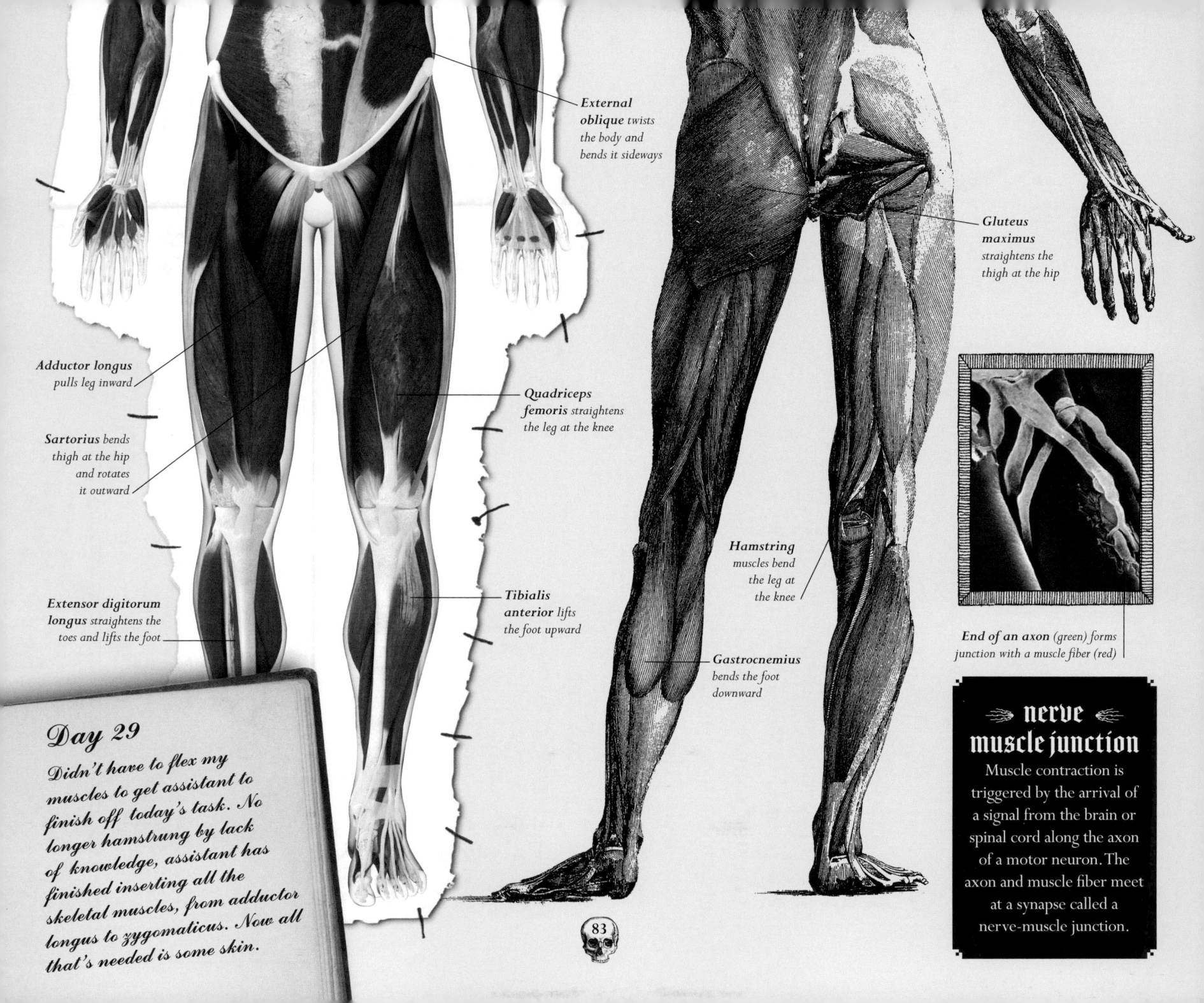
External oblique twists the body and bends it sideways
Gluteus maximus straightens the thigh at the hip
Adductor longus pulls leg inward
Quadriceps femoris straightens the leg at the knee
Sartorius bends thigh at the hip and rotates it outward
Hamstring muscles bend the leg at the knee
Extensor digitorum longus straightens the toes and lifts the foot
Tibialis anterior lifts the foot upward
Gastrocnemius bends the foot downward
End of an axon (green) forms junction with a muscle fiber (red)
Day 29
Didn't have to flex my muscles to get assistant to finish off today's task. No longer hamstrung by lack of knowledge, assistant has finished inserting all the skeletal muscles, from adductor longus to zygomaticus. Now all that's needed is some skin.
nerve muscle junction
Muscle contraction is triggered by the arrival of a signal from the brain or spinal cord along the axon of a motor neuron. The axon and muscle fiber meet at a synapse called a nerve-muscle junction.

Skin, hair, and nails

Now we must cover our body with skin to protect its delicate tissues. This living overcoat is flexible, self-repairing, waterproof, and germ-proof. It also filters harmful rays in sunlight. Your skin can sense touch, pressure, heat, cold, and pain. It also helps the body to maintain a steady internal temperature.

two layers

The epidermis, the skin's upper layer, is its protective part. Its uppermost cells are packed with the waterproof protein keratin, also found in hair and nails. The dermis, the lower, thicker layer, has a blood supply, sweat glands, nerves, sensory endings, and hair follicles.

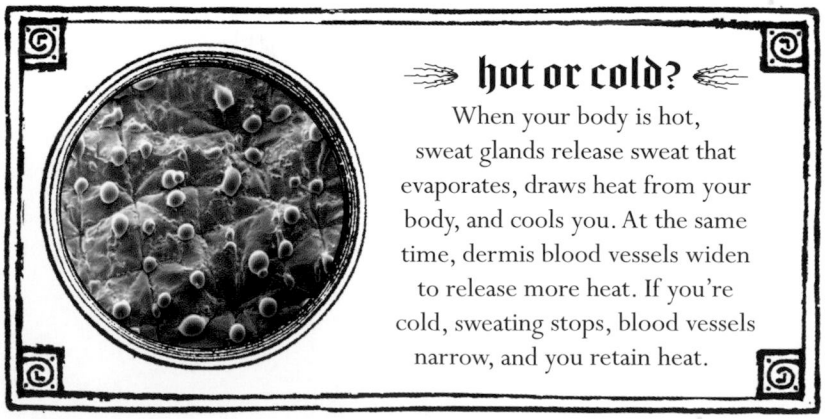

hot or cold?

When your body is hot, sweat glands release sweat that evaporates, draws heat from your body, and cools you. At the same time, dermis blood vessels widen to release more heat. If you're cold, sweating stops, blood vessels narrow, and you retain heat.

Epidermis *is upper layer of the skin*

Hair shaft *is made of dead, keratin-filled cells*

Nerve ending *that detects light touch*

Hair follicle *is cavity from which hair grows*

Sebaceous gland *produces oily sebum*

Hair bulb *contains living cells that divide to make hair grow*

Fat *under the dermis insulates the body*

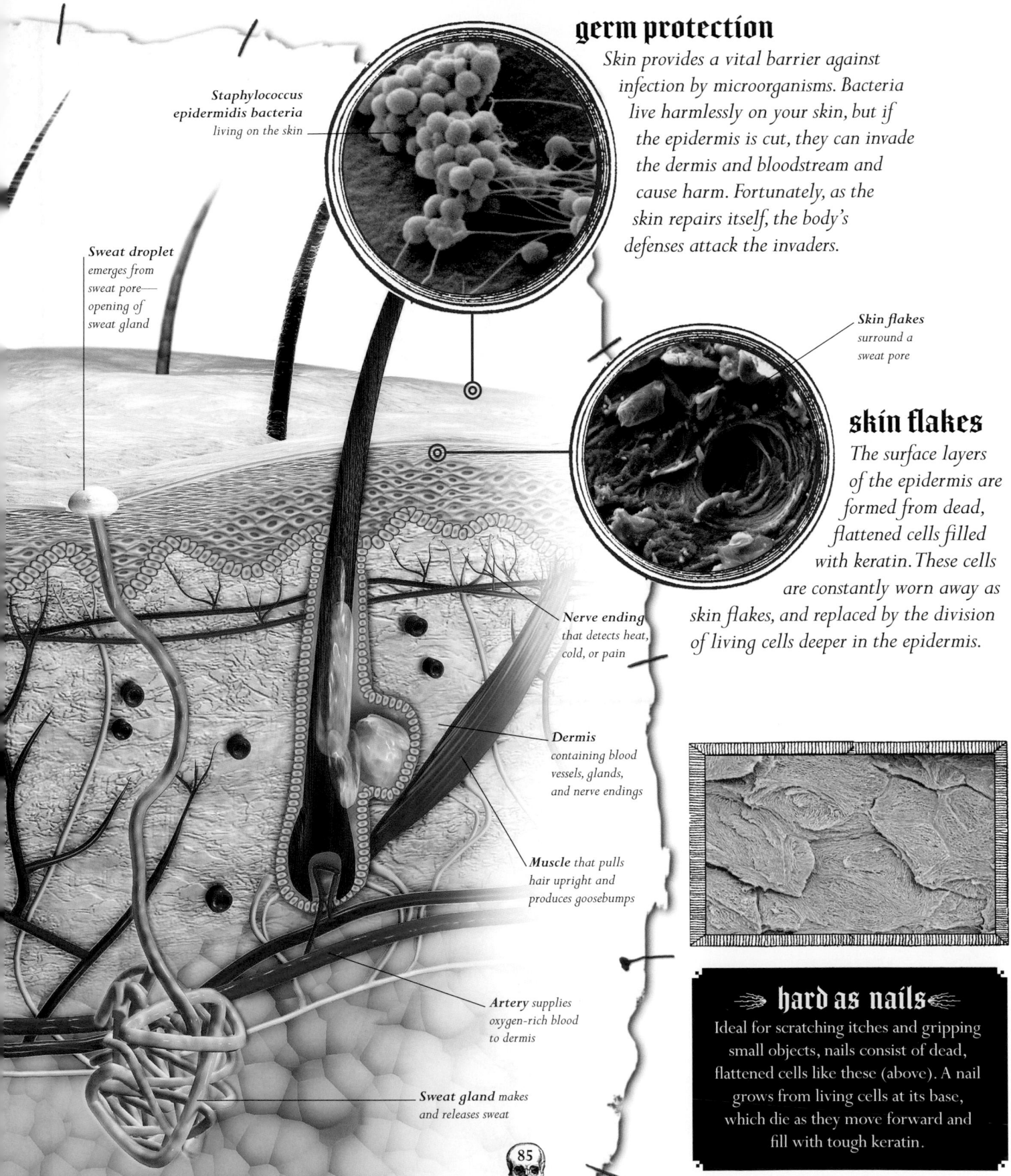

germ protection

Skin provides a vital barrier against infection by microorganisms. Bacteria live harmlessly on your skin, but if the epidermis is cut, they can invade the dermis and bloodstream and cause harm. Fortunately, as the skin repairs itself, the body's defenses attack the invaders.

skin flakes

The surface layers of the epidermis are formed from dead, flattened cells filled with keratin. These cells are constantly worn away as skin flakes, and replaced by the division of living cells deeper in the epidermis.

hard as nails

Ideal for scratching itches and gripping small objects, nails consist of dead, flattened cells like these (above). A nail grows from living cells at its base, which die as they move forward and fill with tough keratin.

The complete body

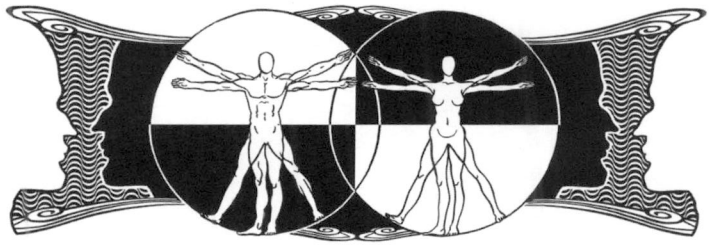

beating heart

How can you tell whether the heart is beating? The quickest way is to feel for a pulse—a surge of blood that's being pumped along an artery running close to the skin's surface.

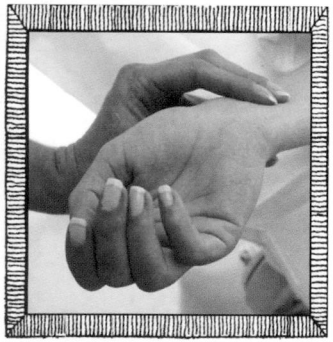

Put two fingers together on the wrist, below the thumb, to feel the pulse.

Congratulations! With your invaluable help, we've managed to assemble a complete living, breathing human being. Let's reflect on this fantastic achievement. We'll take a look at the parts we've assembled and run some tests to check that everything's working.

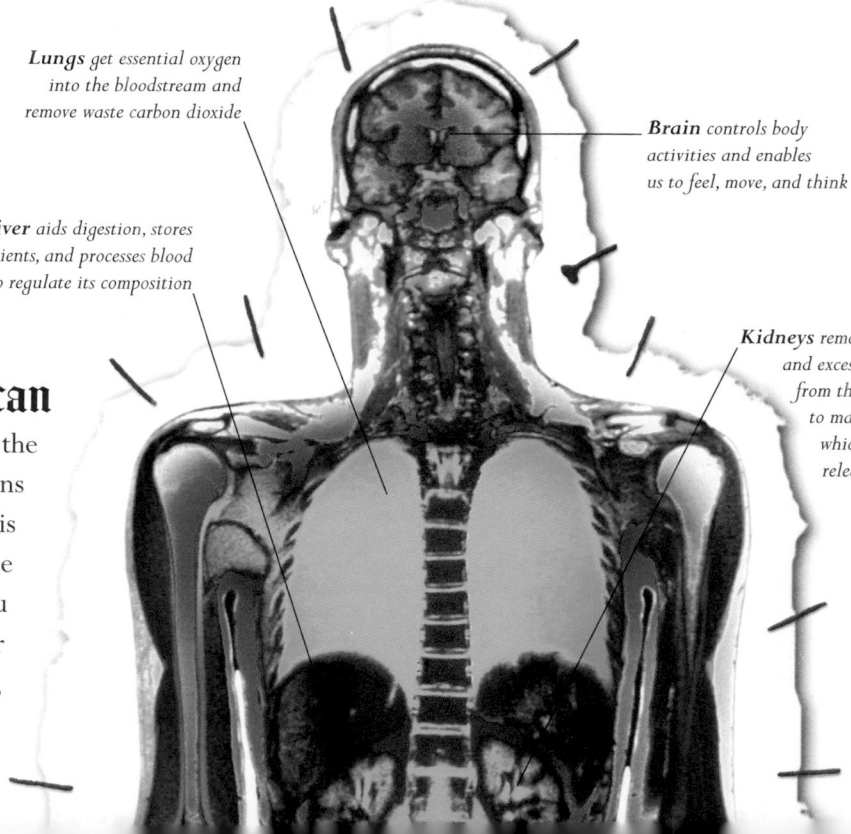

whole body scan

There's no need to pull the body apart to review the organs that we've added. Instead, this remarkable MRI scan shows the insides of the human body. You can see some of the body's major components, including bones, muscles, lungs, and the brain.

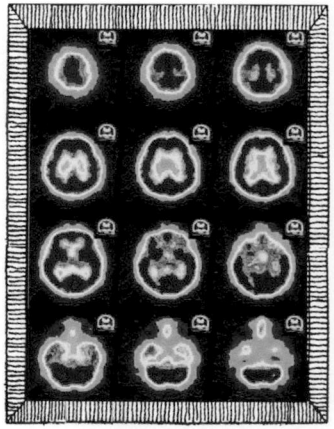

busy brain

A single photon emission computed tomography (SPECT) scan uses tiny amounts of a radioactive substance to show brain activity. In this scan (above), horizontal slices through the brain are shown at different levels. Red areas are the most active.

on the move

Working together, your senses, brain, spinal cord, nerves, and muscles control your every move, from clicking on the television remote control to leaping in the air. The harder your muscles work, the more heat they release. You can see this heat as the red color in this thermogram.

Day 30

The atmosphere is electric. In just one month, assistant and I have succeeded in constructing a human body. I've decided to call it Boris. Am thinking assistant, Boris, and I should take a break from the laboratory and go on a vacation. We're all exhausted!

Quadriceps femoris *is powerful thigh muscle that straightens the leg at the knee*

Femur*, the largest bone in the skeleton, supports the body's weight during standing, walking, and running*

system check

Earlier you discovered that tissues make organs, and organs link up to form 12 body systems. Now the systems are in place, you need to remember that they work together. For example, the circulatory system supplies every organ with oxygen and food obtained by the respiratory and digestive systems.

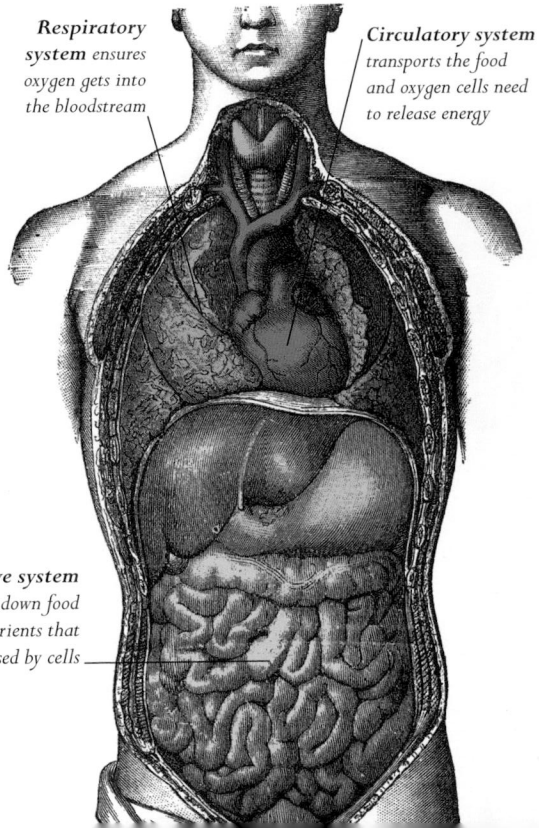

Seeing inside

Throughout this project I have used various techniques—some old, some new—to check on the structure and workings of cells, tissues, and organs. You will have seen X-rays, angiograms, and MRI scans among the variety of images. Now I've got a little time to explain how these images are produced.

X-ray machine

When X-rays were discovered in 1895 by Wilhelm Roentgen, they had an immediate impact. For the first time, doctors could see bones without cutting open the body. X-rays are still used in hospitals today.

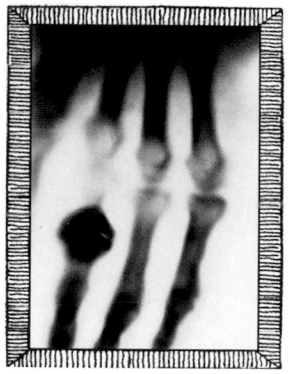

Early X-ray showing Mrs. Roentgen's finger bones and a ring.

Vacuum tube *produces X-rays*

Cable *carries electricity to vacuum tube*

Early X-ray machine *attached to adjustable framework*

Handle *adjusts height and angle of vacuum tube*

Patient entering CT scanner.

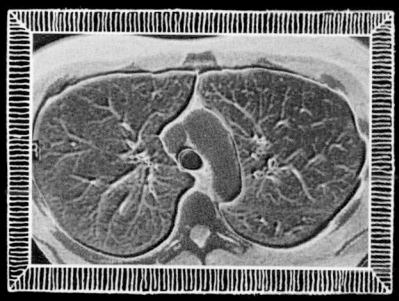

"Slice" through chest shows lungs (blue).

CT scan

As a person lies inside a computed tomography (CT) scanner, a rotating X-ray beam passes through the body into a detector. A computer analyzes the signals and produces a picture of tissues as a slice or a 3-D image.

MRI scan

This method of looking at tissues uses magnets and radio waves to produce detailed sections through the body. In this magnetic resonance imaging (MRI) scan of the head and neck you can clearly see the cerebrum (red) and part of the spinal cord (yellow) running through the backbone.

Backbone *supports the body and forms a protective tunnel around spinal cord*

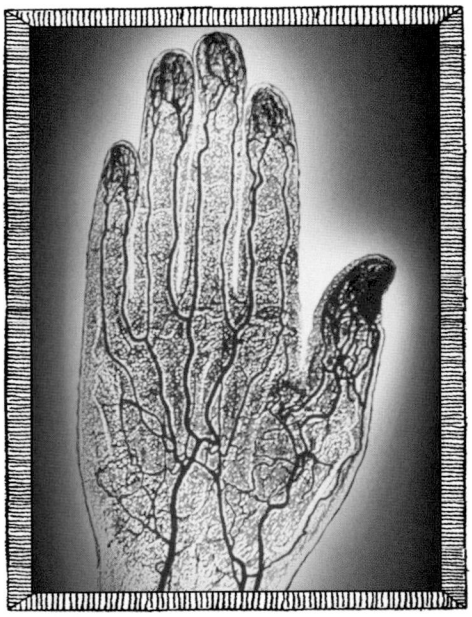

angiogram

Ordinary X-rays don't show up soft tissues. By introducing a special dye into blood vessels, however, these tissues can be seen in X-rays called angiograms. This angiogram (above) shows the arteries in the hand.

bone scan

Radionuclide (gamma) scans show where bones are most active. A special fluid that emits a type of radioactivity is injected into the body. The most active cells take up the radionuclide and emit more gamma rays. In this scan of the feet, areas where bone cells are very active appear red or white.

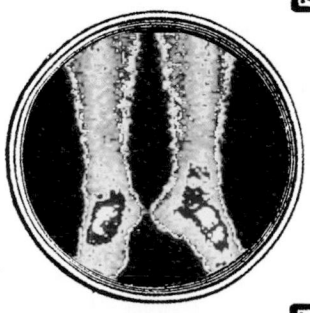

Glossary

abdomen
The part of the body between the chest and the hips.

alimentary canal
The tube that extends from the mouth to the anus.

antibody
A substance released by the immune system that marks a pathogen.

artery
A blood vessel that carries blood away from the heart toward the tissues.

atom
The smallest part of a pure substance.

atrium
One of two upper heart chambers.

autonomic nervous system
The part of the nervous system that automatically controls certain activities, such as heart rate and sweating.

axon
A long, thin part extending from a neuron that carries nerve signals to another neuron.

bacteria
Microorganisms that can cause disease.

carbon dioxide
A gas released by cells as a waste product.

cardiac muscle
A type of muscle found only in the heart.

cartilage
A type of connective tissue that supports the body.

cell
One of the many microscopic living units from which the body is built.

cerebral cortex
The surface layer of the cerebrum, the largest part of the brain.

dendrite
A short process that extends from a neuron and receives signals from other neurons.

digestion
The breakdown of complex molecules in food into simple nutrients that can be used by the body.

DNA (deoxyribonucleic acid)
A molecule found inside the nucleus of a cell that carries instructions (genes) on how the cell should work.

endocrine system
A collection of glands that release hormones into the bloodstream.

enzyme
A protein that accelerates the rate of chemical reactions.

fat
A substance that supplies energy and insulates the body.

feces
The semisolid waste left at the end of digestion.

gland
A group of cells that produce and release substances.

glucose
A sugar that is the main source of energy for body cells.

hormone
A chemical messenger released by an endocrine gland to control certain body activities.

immune system
The system of defense cells that track and destroy pathogens to protect the body against disease.

joint
A place where two or more bones meet.

ligament
A tough strap of connective tissue that holds bones together at joints.

microorganism
A living thing that can only be seen with a microscope.

molecule
A tiny particle made from two or more atoms.

nephron
One of the tiny filtration units in the kidneys that make urine.

neuron
A nerve cell that transmits electrical signals.

nutrient
A substance in food that provides cells with energy and materials for growth and repair.

organ
A body part made of tissues that has a specific role.

oxygen
A gas used by cells to release energy.

pathogen
A microorganism that causes disease.

protein
One of a group of substances that perform many roles, including as enzymes and antibodies.

skeletal muscle
A type of muscle that is attached to bones and moves the body.

smooth muscle
A type of muscle found in hollow organs that contracts slowly and rhythmically to move something.

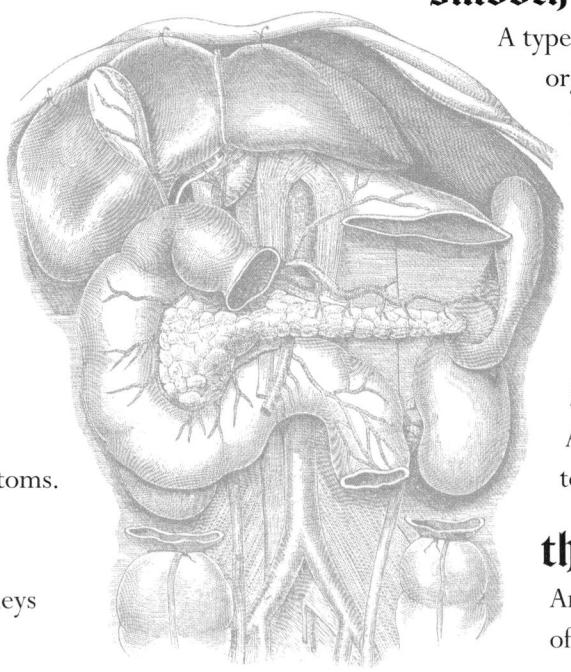

sphincter
A ring of muscle that controls the flow of liquid through an opening.

system
A group of linked organs that work together to perform a specific role.

thermogram
An image that shows the amount of heat released by parts of the body.

tissue
A community of cells that work together.

vein
A blood vessel that carries blood toward the heart.

ventricle
One of two lower heart chambers.

X-ray
A technique that uses a form of radiation and photographic film to produce images of bones and other dense tissues.

Index

A page number in **bold** refers to the main entry for that subject

A

adipose tissue 13
adrenal gland 52
alimentary canal 58–63
ankles 27
appendix 67
arms **20–21**, 76–77
arteries 42, 50–51, 89
atoms 10
autonomic nervous system 40
axons 34, 35,83

B

backbone **16–17**
bacteria 56, 67, 85
balance 38, 39
bile 64, 65
bladder 54, 55
blood **44–45**, 51
blood cells:
  red 15, 44, 45
  white 45, 49
blood clots 44
blood vessels 13, **42–43**, 50, 51
bone 13, **14–15**, 89
  injuries 21, 23, 27
bone marrow 15, 45
brain **30–31**, 32–33, 34, 40, 86
breathing 74, 75
bronchi **70–71**, 72, 75
bronchioles 72, 75

C

capillaries 43
carbon dioxide 72, 74
cartilage 13, 18, 23
cells 10, 11
central nervous system **32–33**
cerebrum **30–31**, 32, 37, 89
circulatory system 50, 87
cochlea 39
colon 62, 63, 67
connective tissue 13
control systems **40–41**

D

dentine 57
diaphragm 74, 75
digestive system 58–65, **66–67**, 87
DNA 11
duodenum 60, 62, 64

E

ears **38–39**
elbows 21, 29
enamel 56
endocrine system 40, 41
enzymes 11, 62, 66
epidermis 12, 84, 85
epiglottis 59, 74
epithelium 12, 13
esophagus **58–59**, 67, 74
expressions 80
eyes **36–37**, 81

F, G

face 19, 80
feces 62, 63
feet **26–27**, 29, 79
fingers 22–23, 77
gall bladder 65
gastric juice 61
genes 11
glands 13, 41, 61

H

hair **84–85**
hands **22–23**, 29, 76–77, 89
heart **46–47**, 50, 51, 72, 75
heartbeat 47
hemoglobin 44, 45
hips 24–25, 29, 78
hormones 41, 52, 65

I, J, K

immune system 49
intestines **62–63**, 66, 67
jaw 18, 81
joints 20, 21, 22, 23, 24, 26, 82
  artificial 25
keratin 84, 85
kidneys **52–53**, 54
knees 26

L

larynx **70–71**, 74
legs **26–27**, 29, 78–79
lens 36
ligaments 21
limbic system 33
liver **64–65**, 67
lungs 50, 70–71, **72–73**
lymphatic system **48–49**, 51
lymph nodes **48–49**

M

microscopes 10
molecules 10
mouth **58–59**, 66
movement 13, 87
muscle fibers 81
muscles 13, 76–81, **82–83**

N

nails **85**
nasal cavity **68–69**, 74
nerves 13, **34–35**, 37, 57, 83
nervous system 32–33, 40, 41
neurons 30, 34, 35
nose **68–69**, 74

O

optic nerves 37

organelles 11
organs **12–13**, 87
ossicles 38, 39
oxygen 10, 68, 72, 74, 75

P

pancreas 62, **64–65**
pathogens 44, 48, 49, 50, 69
pelvis **24–25**
pituitary gland 41
proteins 11
pulse 42, 86
pupils 36

R

raw materials **10–11**
reflexes 33
reproductive system 55
respiratory system 68–73, **74–75**, 87
ribs **16–17**, 73

S

salivary glands 59, 66
scans 86, 88, 89
shoulders **20–21**, 28
sinuses 18, 69
skeleton 16–27, **28–29**
skin 12, **84–85**
skull **18–19**, 28
sleep 41
smell 69
sneezing 74
spinal cord 33, 89
spine 16–17
stomach 12, 59, **60–61**, 67
sweating 84
synapse 35
systems 12, 13, 87

T

taste 58
teeth **56–57**, 59
temperature 78, 84
tendons 77
thighs 26, 78
throat **58–59**
thumb 22
tissues **12–13**
tongue 58
trachea **70–71**, 75
transportation systems **50–51**

U, V

ureter 53, 55
urinary system 53, **54–55**
valves 46, 48
veins 42, 50–51
vertebrae 16, 33
villi 62
voice box 70

W, X

water 10, 63
windpipe 70
wrist 22, 77
X-rays 88, 89

Acknowledgments

Dorling Kindersley would like to thank Chris Bernstein for the index.

Picture Credits
The publisher would like to thank the following for their kind permission to reproduce their photographs:

(Key: a-above; b-below/bottom; c-center; l-left; r-right; t-top)

Alamy Images: Scott Camazine 21cl; Kari Marttila 21br; Dennis Kunkel/PHOTOTAKE Inc. 68bl; DK Images: Geoff Brightling, courtesy of Denoyer-Geppert Intl. 42-43; Mary Evans Picture Library: 8-9; Science & Society Picture Library: 88l; Science Photo Library: 13cra, 23br, 46ca, 46cl, 54bc, 54bl, 80bl; Anatomical Travelogue 33b; Francis LeRoy, Biocosmos 44c; Kenneth Eward/Biografx 66t; Biophoto Associates 12cl; Dr. Arnold Brody 73t; BSIP 25t; BSIP Edwige 88tr; BSIP, Chassenet 36l; BSIP, Humbert/Amel. Magali 86b; CNRI 38bl, 49tc, 52bl, 53t, 70c, 89br; Brad Nelson/Custom Medical Stock Photo 53br; Richard Wehr/Custom Medical Stock Photo 84l; Robert Becker/Custom Medical Stock Photo 15cr; Gregory Dimijian 37br; Du Cane Medical Imaging Ltd 23bl; Brian Evans 55tr; Dr. Tim Evans 11tr; Eye of Science 49br, 56tl, 62tl, 85cr; Simon Fraser 50tr, 86-87c; GCa 19bl; David Gifford 26cb; GJLP 16cb, 33ca; GJLP/CNRI 89; Pascal Goetgheluck 68tl; Gustoimages 22c, 27clb; Adam Hart-Davis 78ca, 78t; Institut Paoli-Calmettes, ISM 28tl; Helene Fournie, ISM 55br; ISM 86t; Jean Abitbol, ISM 70bl, 70br; P. Sole, ISM 11br; Sovereign, ISM 41tl; Astrid Kage 65cr; Manfred Kage 47br, 55bl, 57br; Mehau Kulyk 32bc, 33cb, 89l; Lunagrafix 67br; David M. Martin, MD 59r, 62c, 63cr, 71cr; Miriam Maslo 27br; Tony McConnell 87b; Astrid & Hanns-Frieder Michler 58br; Hank Morgan 31br, 41br, 41crb; Don Fawcett 35b, 83t; Prof. P. Motta/Dept. of Anatomy/University "'La Sapienza," Rome 42bl, 42br, 58tl, 63br, 64l, 65bl, 65tr; Professors P. Motta & T. Naguro 69c; Professors P.M. Motta, P.M. Andrews, K.R. Porter & J. Vial 81b; Steve Gschmeissner 12bl, 13bl, 13crb, 15tr, 30br, 34l, 38c, 39tl, 48c, 49cb, 52tr, 59bl, 62bl, 71tr, 82t; C. J. Guerin, PhD, MRC Toxicology Unit 31tr; National Cancer Institute 45cr; Susumu Nishinaga 15tl, 36c, 39br, 39tr, 43tr, 44b, 61bl, 64c, 69l, 85br; Omikron 37cr; Alfred Pasieka 18cl, 20bl, 28bl, 72bl, 88br; Ed Reschke/Peter Arnold Inc 55tl; Phantomotix 10cl; Philippe Plailly 46cb; Russell Kightley 11l; Dept. of Clinical Radiology, Salisbury District Hospital 21ca; David Scharf 85t; Dr. K. F. R. Schiller 60c; SCIMAT 56br; Dr. Gary Settles 74bl; Andrew Syred 14br; Arthur Toga/UCLA 33tl; Victor Habbick Visions 10cr; M. I. Walker 48b; Zephyr 17tl, 40b, 43tl, 67bl, 73cr, 74t
Historical images from the title "Medical and Anatomical Illustrations," edited by Jim Harter, courtesy of Dover Publications.

All other images © Dorling Kindersley
For further information see: www.dkimages.com

Every effort has been made to trace all copyright holders. The publishers will be pleased to hear from any copyright holders not here acknowledged.

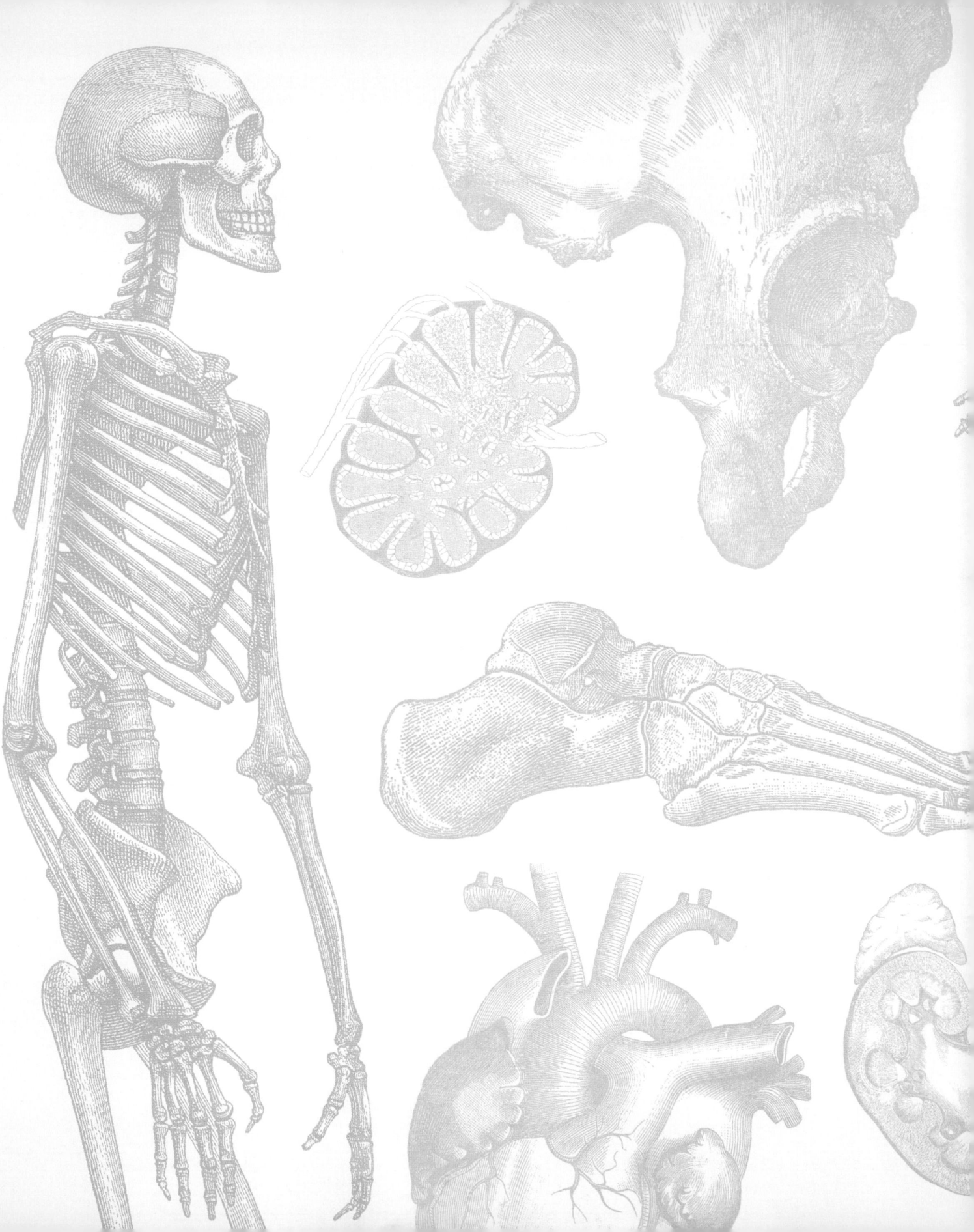

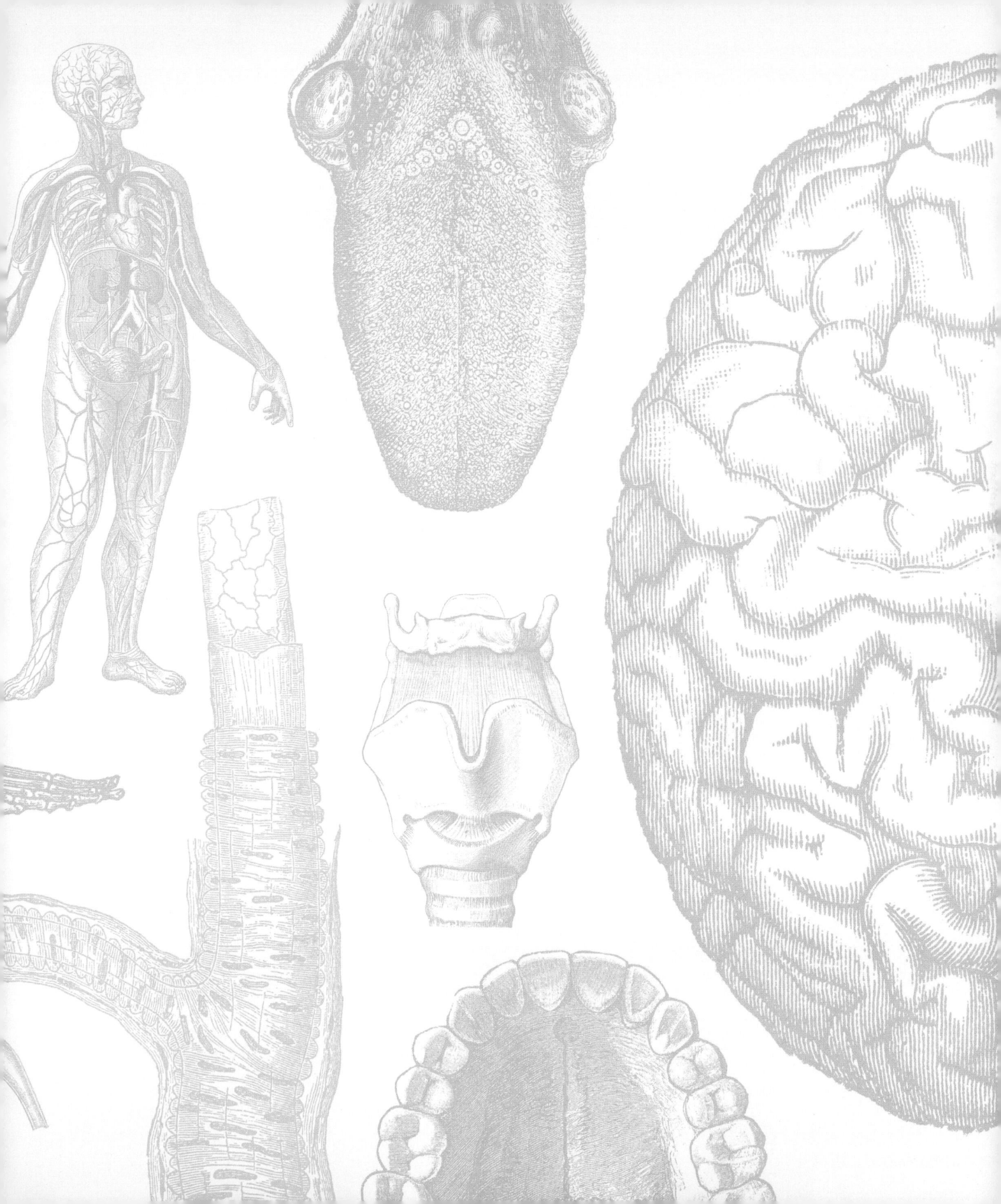